ACBC

- (After Corona Before Corona)

L Ravindran

Tara Ravindran

DEDICATION

To all our dear medical and healthcare professionals and to the Governments of the world and to the citizens who overcame this crisis, with an experience of a lifetime.

EPIGRAPH

The secret of happiness is to face the fact that the world is horrible- Bertrand Russell

He who has a why to live, can bear almost anyhow – Friedrich Nietzsche

That it will never come again is what makes life so sweet – Emily Dickinson

It will never rain roses when we want, to have more roses, we must plant more trees – T.S. Eliot

The world is so constructed that if you wish to enjoy its pleasures, you must also endure its pains – St. Teresa of Avila

Wisdom comes only through suffering – Aeschylus

When all else is lost, the future still remains – Bower

CONTENTS

L Ravindran and Tara Ravindran

FOREWORD

by K. Jairaj, I.A.S,

RETIRED ADDITIONAL CHIEF SECRETARY,
GOVERNMENT OF KARNATAKA, INDIA.

The Covid-19 crisis has caught all of us with surprise and unresolved fears. Our lives were severely disrupted by the nationwide lockdown announced from the third week of March,2020.

Uncertainty set in when we witnessed the unabated prevalence of the virus starting from China spreading all over the world, especially the West and the United States. Human misery increased exponentially in our country especially regarding the vulnerable sections of society, notably the distress caused to migrant labor and those subsisting on daily wages who had lost their means of employment.

While others may have hunkered down and tried to adjust to the new regimen of being at home, the authors of this book- the energetic couple of Dr. Ravindran and Mrs. Tara Ravindran have put the time to good use. Their book ACBC is an enquiry on the ongoing pandemic and the changes that mankind have resorted to, to adapt to a better tomorrow by learning from the challenges of staying indoors and operating in an alien environment.

Most Governments, as we see are equally bewildered, and have been left blinded, not knowing how to deal with the crisis. The NDRF (National Disaster Response Force), a unique force in India set up to monitor crises of any kind did not foresee a micro-organism playing havoc both in the minds and physically too, debilitating one's health without sparing even the medical professionals who became a major victim and feared the disease.

Well industrialized nations too with all their financial might were left exposed. We are back to the square one. We could not have imagined clear blue skies, chirping of birds, wild animals moving around on roads in the absence of cars and vehicles and closed commercial spaces for 8-10 weeks around the world.   Production of goods and services and productivity has been impacted dearly. Entrepreneurs, businessmen and Government together are trying to salvage the situation and jump start into a new beginning.

Dr Ravindran (Ravi) and Mrs. Tara Ravindran are uniquely placed to come out with this book. Both have had substantive work backgrounds and a wide array of interests characterizing their lives.

Ravi is a full-fledged Corporate professional and institutional builder, deeply interested in academic matters having acquired a Ph.D. as well and interested in the leading economic and technological issues of the day. Tara, on the other hand, trained in interior science, has been a teacher, motivator, coach and with abiding interest in social issues. Together, they are an ideal couple complementing each other and this book is another example.

In this book, the authors have given brief ideas and their observations on every possible cluster and occupations and have also visualized how the industrial and work environment could be changing so as to stay relevant. A comparison is also made amongst many nations as to how they are protecting businesses and salaried classes. The poor and the vulnerable, the young and unemployed also find solace in few Government schemes. Poor, hunger, salvation, livelihoods are to get their due attention.

Capitalist nations, for once have become socialists. Migrants, have got sandwiched in our nation or when settled in a foreign land. Not knowing the origin, countries around the world are reforming to more protectionist norms. The world, in the eyes of the authors will undergo significant changes and the book with many economic factors and analysis may become a ready reckoner for one to quickly refer to as to what each of us did to stave off the crisis in a miniature form. I Commend the authors for their efforts in educating us about the Pandemic and sharing their views on how to visualize the future, with hope and optimism.

K JAIRAJ

ACKNOWLEDGMENT

In God we trust and would thank Panchamukhi Hanuman and Raghavendra Swami ji.

We remain grateful to our parents and all our immediate family members, our daughter and son-in-law and his parents and to our pet and to our office colleagues.

Our special thanks to Ms. Sharma, Mr. Vinod and their family members for the cover page design.

PREFACE

We are indeed grateful that this book has reached your hands.

ACBC is a book based on the recent learnings and sharing of our experiences which you might have seen it yourself over the last 30 days or so. This is something new to us and yourself.

What we have done here is to visualize the present and factor the future using plain sense- common sense. This book has been written between end March'20 and is out for reading now.

The distractions in terms of participation in few webinars, stretched office work-from-home, personal work catered to at- home, learning to adjust the newfound daily schedules, intense spirituality, philosophical or economical at times, etc.

Lots of reading material when we perused was driving us crazy. Many were shooting in the dark. The best way to stay away from the distraction was to listen to truth or not hear the noise and clutter around us and develop a sense of gloom and doom.

There are many good people who encouraged us, not knowing that we may not be the best writers, but people expressing just common observations for others to fathom. This book drawn with a strong Indian connect and perspective may develop a sense of positivity and can help look at post Covid-19, with a feeling of hope that India will emerge a stronger country, being a strong patriot and an ideal nationalist.

INTRODUCTION

World before 2020 and after 2020 are going to be different. No human will behave as much as s/he used to before Jan'2020. What we are seeing is an unprecedented change, never imagined before.

Man –animal conflicts are on the rise. With continuous destruction of forests and wildlife, human settlements have moved far beyond.

While one plans to go up into MARS, there is a near resonance to go far into forests to claim lost land and inhabitation. The results are there for one to see. Coronavirus is one such example. We have seen, in the past, SARS, Ebola, Swine flu and many more. This may not be the end, but just the beginning.

 Life after corona is bound to be different, multiple reset buttons are likely to be pushed in how we live, socialize, work or entertain. W-F-H (Work-From-Home) could morph from a stop gap arrangement into a tool for cost efficiency.

In times like these human vulnerability faces off between nature (the pandemic) and nurture (economics of making goods and services available to all). Pets are becoming collateral victims of Covid-19.

The pandemic has given us a different perspective on things we considered important. Now, we ask the question: Are they really important?

Life has come a full circle and we now believe existence is God's Gift and we would remain eternally happy with the most basic necessities.

We seem to have gone round to get back to basics. What was once taught to us as good hygiene factors have resurfaced now. These used to be our childhood habits, to wash our hands and legs before entering our homes, upon return from work or play. All of us come out with 'balancing realism with steadfast optimism' defined with endurance and survival as said by Jim Collins in his book Good to Great, where he talks about Stockdale paradox named after Admiral Stockdale who overcame the Vietnam War as a prisoner of war for 7 years.

Be it for Gen Z (1995-2015), Gen Y (1980-94), Gen X (1965-80), Baby- boomer (1944-64), Older generation born before 1944, the result is for everyone to see.

CHAPTER-1
WORLDWIDE VIEW, DEEPER LOOK INTO INDIA – BEFORE AND AFTER CORONA

More than 2500 years ago, Lord Buddha set out on a journey to find out why one suffers. He discovered that there are 3 basic facts of all existence:

1. Anicca, impermanence, or change;
2. Dukkha, suffering and
3. Anatta, non self.

The first and third apply to inanimate existence as well, while the second is an experience of the animate like us.

Anicca, which is at the core of Buddha's teachings means that reality is never static, but is dynamic.

The truth of impermanence helps us to develop 2 vital mental qualities:

a. **Equanimity**: helps us to end or mitigate suffering. Bereft of ego, it helps us to handle highs and lows, with equipoise and calmness. This attitude helps us to cope with the stress, frustration and despair that may arise out of impermanence.
b. **Empathy:** helps us to internalise impermanence. Identifying and reaching out to those in greater pain, agony and suffering is a fine act of humanity.

Goodwill, fellow feeling, helps us to deal with the turbulence of impermanence with a deep sense of togetherness.[1] This pandemic has exposed our vulnerabilities as supposedly great savers. Liquidity is heavily constrained when it is most desirable.

World Population and their engagements

Approximately, out of 7 billion that the world has as its population, the elderly (0.577 billion) and the unemployed (0.43 billion) totals to about 1 billion, which is roughly 14% of the world population. Another 1.9 billion are children.

This in effect means that the financially productive population is 59% who are employed in services (1.7 billion), agriculture (1.4 billion), industrial works (0.8 billion) and entrepreneurship including professionals and self- employed (0.4 billion). Services, agriculture, industrial workers totally work out to 3.9 billion.

Currently, the world has about 7.9 billion as its population and out of this about 3. 7 lakh persons succumbed to corona virus (infected are 6 million with the numbers growing every passing day). Amongst the worst hit, the USA, has accounted for 1/4th followed by UK, Italy, Brazil, France, Spain. The numbers in India are increasing.

---

[1] Sahu Ramkrishna, Article, Economic Times, 02/05/2020

Figure 1- What do 7 billion population do in this world- (figs.in billion)

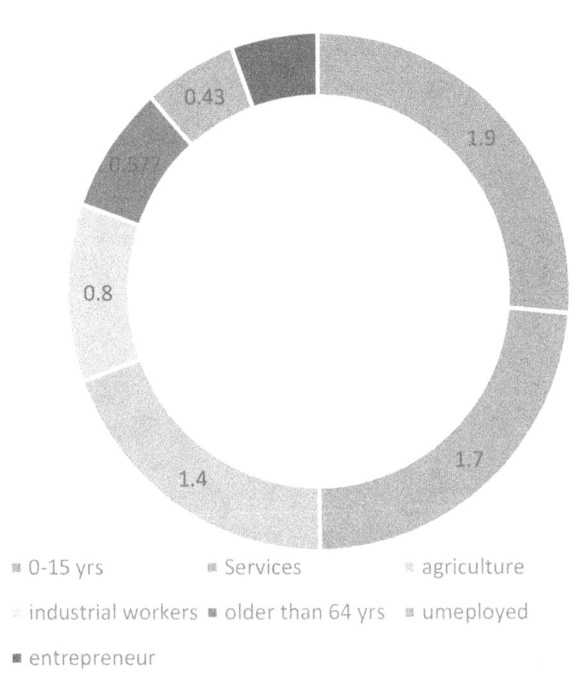

Source: cia.gov; census.gov; gemconsortium.org

The 2 pandemics that afflict us in related but distinct ways

There are 2 pandemics in play now: one is the Covid-19 and the other is the pandemic of anxiety about the economic consequences of the first as per Robert J Shiller, a Nobel laureate in economics, professor at Yale University, and the author of 'Irrational Exuberance'.

The anxiety is the unfolding crisis and how it can trample upon our hard earned savings and the lifestyle changes that we may need to undergo at this juncture. One does not know what action to take.

Concerns like unemployment, business closures, loss of income are the matters which may make one desperate for work, from taking adequate precautions against the spread of the disease. However, one can solace from the fact that the recession is universal.

Psychologist, Paul Slovic of the University of Oregon calls this phenomenon as "affect heuristic". When people are emotionally disturbed because of a tragic event, they react with fear in circumstances where there is no reason to fear.

A contagion of financial anxiety works differently, than a contagion of disease. It is fueled in part by people noticing others lack of confidence, reflected in price declines, and other emotional reaction to the declines. A negative bubble in the stock market occurs when people see prices falling and trying to discover why, then they start amplifying stories that explain the decline. Then, prices fall on subsequent days, and again and again.

After observing successive decreases in stock prices one gets a powerful feeling of regret for those who have not sold, together with a fear that one might sell at the bottom. This regret and fear prime people's interest in both pandemic narratives.

Generally, people believe that all economic crisis is the banking crisis that has got unraveled. This time, there is no fear of a banking crisis so wait and watch is the attitude of many. Moreover, in the last 2 decades we have possibly overcome 2 or more crises and come out triumphant in the next 5-7 years.

In the past, not many people invested in the stock markets and not many relied on these instruments for their retirement as inflation was seemingly low. The longevity, post retirement was relatively much lower.

Predicting the outcome of the pandemic and its effects on the stock market is a difficult call on which neither economists nor financial analysts are well prepared.

What is the new normal, reboot and reset buttons?

The month-long lockdown has achieved many a fascinating matter which were inconceivable and that would have otherwise taken years to achieve.

Our country at most times was considered a Third world country. Most of us seem to live in grand places inside a villa / compound and chose to ignore outside of it except when being on the road.

The last one month has made every place in India to be on par with the First world with clean air, cleaner roads, clear blue sky, better air quality, etc. to name a few. This is the change in the making and adoption of India into the First World. Can this remain a fantasy or a dream come true? All of us including the policy makers have a role to play here.

Every morning we wake up to the sounds of the birds and cuckoos which became invisible not long ago. The common sparrow and crows became uncommon.

Lockdown has also made our middle class and the upper class in the society to change their practices and behaviors. With our regular cooks and maids unavailable, cooking and mopping for downtime or for relaxing or for pleasure has become a necessity – much like those living in western world or the First World. The DIY (Do-It-Yourself) norms match with the First World, except that they are more mechanized than India.

The Covid-19 has given rise to the speculation that First World conditions are not inherently, intrinsically impossible in "Third World '2020, India[2]. Let us hope the lockdown brings us closer or into the First World itself. Swatch Bharat will be a gainer.

What we are evidencing is not a relative shock but an aggregate shock?[3]

An economics professor at IIMB, Vivek Moorthy, explains the difference that a relative shock is suffered when car owners suddenly switch over from petrol to diesel vehicles. The total distance driven may not change much as a consequence.

But, when demand for all forms of travel collapses, that is aggregate shock. Countries and States, locked their population from the neighbor states and countries in order to protect their citizens and to ward off the Corona virus. What may stick in our mind is our impermanence, post the lockdown and the remedy that becomes available sometime in the future.

---

[2] Hazra Indrajit, Article, Economic Times, 25/04/20

[3] Khanna Sundeep, Article, Mint

ACBC – (After Corona Before Corona)

The New Normal

After 76 days of isolation, from Jan 23rd to April 8th '2020, Hubei province which had the biggest quarantine in the world ranging between 50-750 million people were at last freed.

People in China find that the shadow of Covid-19 is still hanging over every aspect of their daily life. The fear of a second wave of infections has made authorities to maintain a range of physical distancing measures as a precaution.

For most of us too, this would be the new normal. An April 14 study by Harvard suggests that physical distancing measures are here to stay, perhaps on an on-and –off basis until 2022, because one time lockdowns may not control the pandemic.

Scientists say that once herd-immunity (mass vaccination) is achieved over few years the new normal may be achieved.

An integral part of our day-to-day life will possibly form part of usage of new phrases that are part of our vocabulary:

- Nucleic acid testing
- Social / physical distancing
- Temperature screening

Offices in China decide which of the employee has to go to work while the rest work from home. Offices have started re organizing their teams so that every department is split into several teams, to ensure that one infection does not paralyze the entire department / team. So, a larger sharing of responsibilities, authorities without the fear of losing position / respect has become the order of the day.

Property management companies have started deciding the no of occupants and no of people allowed to enter an office.

Health is no longer a private matter. Only Health QR code can get one an important passport to move around freely in domestic / international travel for any citizen.

An app that every citizen has to download marks you green (safe), while orange or red may mean that you cannot enter a shopping mall or restaurant. The color depends on your travel history and who you have been in contact with, among other things.

Corporate survivors from Depression era

Possibly the world will be into an economic contraction matched only by the Great Depression years of 1929 to 1941. That Depression was set off by a stock market collapse of October 1929.

The Smoot- Hawley Act, 1930 led to sharp hike in import tariffs on hundreds of products to protect local producers, leading to over 2/3rd contraction in global trade and an increase in prices of agricultural products in the USA. Even then the hardest of the hardship was faced by the poorest and the marginalized. This is similar to what is happening now during the ongoing pandemic.

In a study in March 2010, in their article titled Roaring out of Recession in the Harvard Business Review (HBR), authors Ranjay Gulati, Nitin Nohria and Franz Wohlgezogen studied 4700 public companies to come up with startling findings: 17% of those companies did not survive a recession and went bankrupt, were acquired or went private. Only a small number of companies about 9% of the sample could flourish after a shutdown.

In a published newspaper article, it is said that "the challenge for companies now will be to join this 9% category, and for that, some lessons[4] learnt from the Depression could come in handy. Here are some lessons gleaned from the business literature of the period.:

1. Spreading love amongst its employees and workforce- According to the HBR study, firms that cut costs faster and deeper than rivals have the lowest likelihood of pulling ahead of the competition when times get better. Instead of letting people go, just imagine the psychological and physical constraints that they are undergoing and still delivering, so would it not be better to expect something beyond the unimaginable?

   A case in point as per Steve Jobs is post the dot com crash, Apple created iTunes and I pod. Post the 2008 financial crisis, Apple launched the I pad in April 2020.

2. Be the customers 3 am friend – The kirana (mom and pop) shop have done wonders by delivering what the super markets and malls have been unable to do so. Once the worst is over, these shops will not be forgotten and they will be deeply valued. Customer memory is deep. If you are not with them today, they will not be with you tomorrow.

3. Unleash the creativity within- Companies who spend higher on marketing efforts will unravel huge benefits and have long standing customers of the future as is understood from the Great Depression era.

4. Take advantage of the "lipstick effect" and provide the "Little Miss sunshine"- This is the time when small luxuries will fill the moods of the consumers. Companies should also show the way out of the current gloom and doom.

5. Be flexible with your business – recessions are the best time to turn convention on its head and look at completely different products and services.

6. Start planning for the next crisis- surely with this, not being the last of the crisis in this world, it is necessary that scenario planning is developed by learning about ones' deficiencies and iron them out so as to stay relevant for the future.

---

[4] Khanna Sundeep, Article, Mint

Worldwide debt

The USA, Japan account for 50% of the worldwide debt. China and India would near about 10%. Worldwide debt in percentage terms is depicted in Figure-2.

Figure 2-World debt (%)

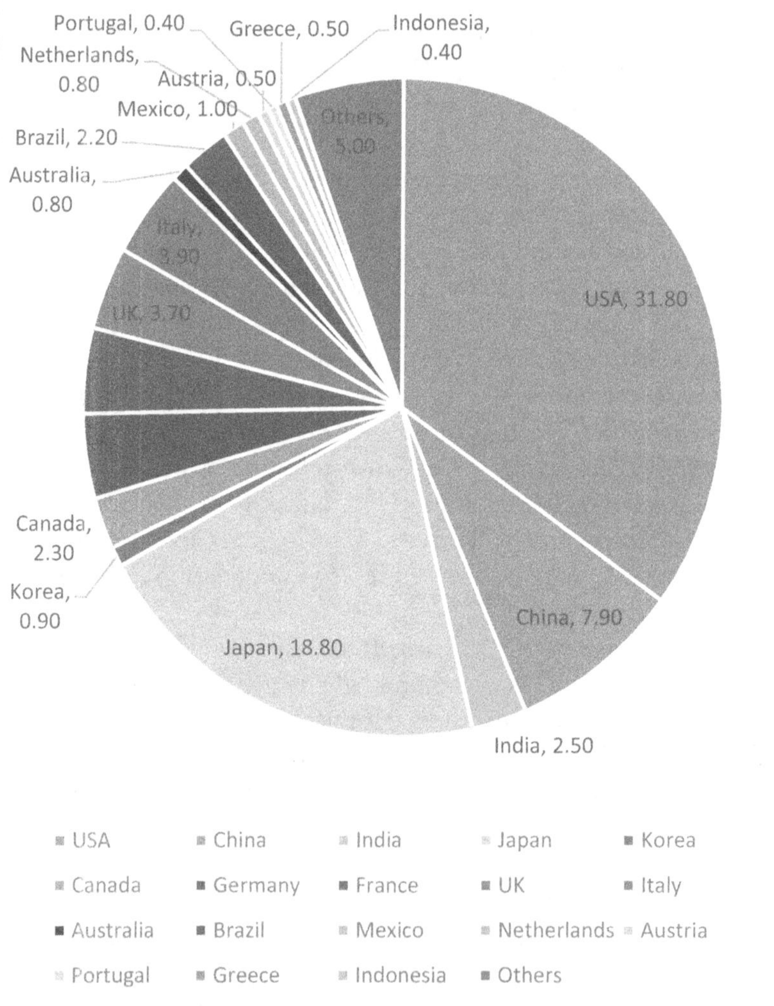

Source: howmuch.net

In nominal terms the US leads the debt by 20 trillion USD of governmental debt. Japan has a sky high debt of 239% of debt to GDP but over 90% of it is held domestically. 40% of the world's debt is accounted for from other countries predominantly Europe.

Countries and their Balancing act

This table below depicts how countries around the world are reducing the stress for employers by supporting their employees.

Table 1- How countries around the world are helping employees and employers

Countries	Measures
Argentina	Employers have to pay salaries for 60 days and not fire workers
Australia	Wage subsidy to businesses of Aus. $ 130 billion (6.5% of GDP)
Austria	State guarantees 90%for gross salaries below 1700 euro, 85% salaries below 5370 euro. Apprentices to be paid in full
Belgium	Help for self-employed. For those in temporary employment, benefits have been raised from 65-70% of gross wages.
Brazil	Informal workers and unemployed will receive over 3 months temporary new benefit of 120 dollars / month under certain conditions
Canada	Canadian dollar 2000 pm, for up to 4 months to those who have lost income due to the pandemic
China	Temporary living allowance for migrant workers and some benefit for jobless
Czech Republic	Quarantined employees to get 60% of salaries while employees in firms which has stopped functioning to be compensated in full
Denmark	State to pay 75% of wages for 3 months if employers do not lay off employees
France	Employees receive an allowance of approximately 84% of net salary. Minimum wage workers to receive 100%
Germany	Employees will tap a Euro 26 billion insurance fund, which guarantees workers at least 60% of their basic pay.
Greece	Allowance of euro 800 for employees of affected companies
Indonesia	Manufacturing workers with annual income below threshold, exempted from income tax for 6 months

Countries	Measures
Ireland	Temporary wage subsidy of 85% (raised from 70% in March) of net weekly take home pay up to Euro 412
Italy	Euro 5 billion top up on wage supplementation scheme for those furloughed employees. Plus one-off payments to various other categories of workers
Japan	All citizens are expected to receive a cash pay-out of 100000 yen ($ 928)
Norway	Provisions for employees who are on temporary lay-off to receive full wage compensation (up to 50000 kroner pm)
Poland	Subsidies for employees' salaries of up to 40% of the average statutory wage, with some conditions
Saudi Arabia	Government will cover 60% of salaries of Saudi staff in companies under stress for next 3 months
Serbia	Payment of 50% of net minimum wage for three months for employees in large private sector companies and for employees who are currently not working
Spain	Affected workers will receive full salary during lockdown. Br on outright dismissals. Plus allowance for temporary workers and household employees
South Korea	Central Government relief cheques to households in the bottom 70% income bracket (around 14 million households), of up to $820 per household.
UK	Income support for families of $1200 for each adult and $ 500 for children, and $ 250 billion to boost unemployment insurance
USA	For 3 months, all employers will get 80% government funding for workers' salaries of up to $ 2500 a month

Source: Economic Times, page -11, 21/04/2020

India's stimulus package

The Government of India brought out a distinctive package, far different from the developed world considering its own limitations. The PM unveiled the Atmanirbhar Bharat (self-reliant India) programme which visualized a grand Rs.20. lakh crores package, most of which is described in Table-2 below. Avoiding macroeconomic instability and inflation for the future, the Government carefully avoided printing of currency but used loans from banks and NBFC's as a vital tool to dole out credit.

ACBC – (After Corona Before Corona)

Table 2- India's measure to cope up with the crisis (as on May15th'2020)

Segment/ Sectors(million benefited)	Measures	Quantum (Rupees. crores.)
Corporates, Businesses	RBI liquidity infusion	804000
MSME's Stressed MSME's Equity for MSME's	Collateral free loan, Government guaranteed Subordinate debt Fund of funds	300000 20000 50000
Power Distribution Companies	Liquidity injection by PFC/ REC with state government guarantee	90000
Farmers (30)	Emergency working capital via NABARD Cheaper credit under kisan credit cards	30000 200000
NBFC's	Partial credit guarantee Special liquidity, security Government guaranteed	45000 30000
Affordable housing (0.25)	Subsidy scheme extended till May'21	70000
Tax payers	TDS/ TCS rate reduced by 25%	50000
Roadside vendors (5)	Working capital of Rs.10000/-	5000
Salaried, workers (formal employment)	PF contribution- employer, employee Lower PF contribution	2500 6750
Job opportunities	States to be funded for afforestation, plantation works	6000
Others	Mudra Shishu loans- payment relief of under Rs.50000 –2% interest subvention	1500
Others	One nation, one ration card	N.A
Banks	Loans guaranteed by Government in many cases	N.A
Agro farming	Bee keeping initiatives Micro food enterprises, cluster based farming Vaccination for rearing of cattle, buffaloes, sheep, goats, pigs Animal husbandry infrastructure	500 10000 13000 15000
	Fish production (aim 70000 tonnes-5 yrs.)	20000
	Agricultural cooperative societies, FPO's, Start-ups- farm gate infrastructure	100000

Sources: various dailies

The poor and needy were served with direct cash transfers while the MNREGS (Mahatma Gandhi National Rural Employment Guarantee Scheme) has an outlay to carry out rural employment for fixed days in a year.

The RBI (Reserve Bank of India) has slashed its Repo rate to 4% while the reverse repo stands at 3.35% and moratorium on debt servicing extended to Aug 31st 2020. Possibly, the Government is treading with caution, by not exercising its full might but holding back its firepower, not knowing how long the fight against Covid-19 will last. There is palpable discontentment though. Many experts feel it has been a policy response more than reforms except in freeing agriculture production and opening up new spaces for FDI.

It is felt by many in India that the poor and migrant workers need cash and not credit. Many policy reforms have been undertaken by the Government utilizing the pandemic as an opportunity to privatize coal, mineral, farming, defense, civil aviation, power, space and atomic energy.

Stimulus package and its effects

Much of India has been disappointed with the stimulus package spelt out by the government which by and large has done a fine balancing act of initiating reforms while keeping expenses under check. No direct compensation has been offered to companies (the employer). With not much of cash put in the hands of the people, it is hard to believe how the economy will see demand revival of goods and services to come out of the recession.

The structural reforms announced can draw investment to make various markets become more efficient but it will take few years to show results.

The Government on its part has allowed loan funding to bear the burden of hauling India's economy out of its deepest slump. Government of India, RBI has opened liquidity windows with some contingency liabilities taken over by the exchequer. Given the weak Balance sheets of lenders, the risk aversion could be higher. The impact on economic outcomes would thus be slow and muted.

The reality of shrunken markets may force companies to delay further investments into their own companies. Most likely companies will downsize their operations and try to reduce debt on their books. With lower demand for borrowing and a toned down commercial activity would see many shrunk balance sheets with lower earnings leading to a compounding of the crisis. India's contraction of GDP is likely to be sharp this year with business confidence getting poorer.

Amid a sell-off in emerging markets this calendar year, Indian Government and corporate bonds totaled $13.7 billion, which sent the rupee to a record low of 76.9088 against the dollar in April. The Indian currency has been among one of Asia's worst performers but has staged a modest recovery since.

The figure below provides the picture of reduction in bond holding by foreign funds in Indian Government bonds.

Figure- 3- Impact on Bond Markets in India

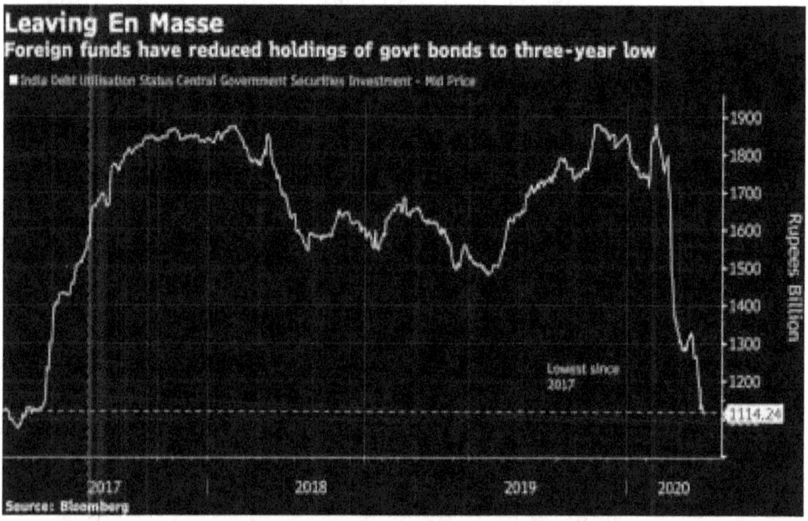

Source: Bloomberg

The sell-off on the bonds places the foreign holding at a three-year low.

Policy Reforms

The Indian Government has utilized the opportunity during the pandemic to bring about several policy reforms, few of which are named here under:

- Health - Public spending to be increased with more health and wellness centres. Infectious diseases and public health labs to be set up in all districts;
- Disinvestment - Public sector firms in non-strategic sectors to be privatised. Not more than 4 PSU's to remain in "strategic sectors".

- State govt. borrowings: ceilings raised from Rs.6.61. lakh crores to Rs.10.69. lakh crores. This is 5% of GSDP (Gross State Domestic Product) raised from 3% of GSDP.
- Unemployment - MGNREGS (Mahatma Gandhi National Rural Employment Guarantee Scheme) - allocation hiked by Rs.40000 crores to fund 300 crores person days, aimed at giving returning migrants an income option.
- Industry - Fresh insolvency proceedings gets suspended for a year, eligible size to be hiked from Rs.1. lakh to Rs.1. crore. Default will not be triggered due to Covid-19 related debts.

Out of Rs.20.97 lakh crores stimulus package - which amounts to 9.8% of GDP - only Rs.2.2. lakh crores can be traced as direct additional budgetary cost to the Central exchequer, while another Rs.1.55. lakh crore relates to already budgetary expenditure. The stimulus dent to fiscal deficit stands at about 1.3% of GDP, say experts. The remaining comes from RBI's liquidity announcements, credit guarantee schemes, insurance schemes, apart from structural reforms which are not really stimulus or relief measures.

What the stimulus package does not address are the following:

1. Business may continue to face stress due to lack of demand;

2. Private consumption is 60% of our economy;

3. Sentiments are down because of job losses / pay cuts across classes;

4. No policy to boost job creation;

5. For low income / unemployed, there is no direct cash support / relief;

6. Consumers will stay cautious due to the uncertain future with

middle income class not deriving benefit;

7. Low demand will continue to pull economy down

Impact on fiscal deficit

As per Abheek Barua, chief economist at HDFC Bank, a large part of the fiscal policy announced above works on guarantees and is not an immediate drag on fiscal resources. SBI's economist, Soumya Kanti Ghosh says that the fiscal stimulus can be funded vide a perpetual sovereign bond, where there is no need to repay back the principal. He feels that the combination of fiscal and monetary stimulus sets off a virtuous cycle of liquidity easing, leading to a reduced level of insolvency with a positive impact on economy. Both of them felt that the Rs.20. lakh crore stimulus announce by our PM will have a muted impact on fiscal deficit and that financing will not be a problem.

CHAPTER-2

LAND & ENVIRONMENT

Agriculture and farming

Much of the rural areas have a better harvest as well as the possibility of a faster economic recovery. This is evident from the loan recoveries even in digital form from rural India while urban India which is dependent upon salaries, job cuts have opted for moratorium payments.

Economists and theorists believe that farm focused activities may rise with a large part of the migrant labor force returning to their native villages from urban centers. With extended lockdown and the quarantine facilities it may become imperative for many to stay back for 6 months and gain productive employment through farming as a means to livelihood. This may boost loan demand from the rural sector for equipment such as tractors. The harvest this year has been good for wheat, sugarcane, pulses and the government may buy and warehouse them. This should further improve cash flows of the farming community.

The Government has added 200 more mandis (open markets) to e NAM (electronic National Agricultural Market) during the pandemic period thus taking the tally to 785 across seven states to its national digital agricultural platform. Farmers have immensely benefited from e NAM where markets were provided to farmers to trade their produce at competitive prices without visiting Mandis during the lockdown period. The number of registered farmers have increased to 1.66. crores while 1.28 lakh traders transact on this platform during end April'20. More than 1000 Farmer Producer Organizations (FPOs) have been enrolled to this platform. Businesses worth over Rs.1. lakh crores have been conducted and helped price discovery mechanism. Very soon, farmers will be able to sell their produce directly to consumer and also have interoperability between state Government platforms and the central governments platform could become a reality thus paving the way for a farmer in Rajasthan to sell his produce in Kerala without travelling to and fro.

Migrant laborers and workers will feel happier to get onto farm production as there is a newfound opportunity. They may decide not to go back to their place of work in larger cities.

Farm to Table and Fork - connect between farmers and ultimate consumers will only increase in the coming years.

India's food grain output

Figure- 4- Staples, food grain output in India

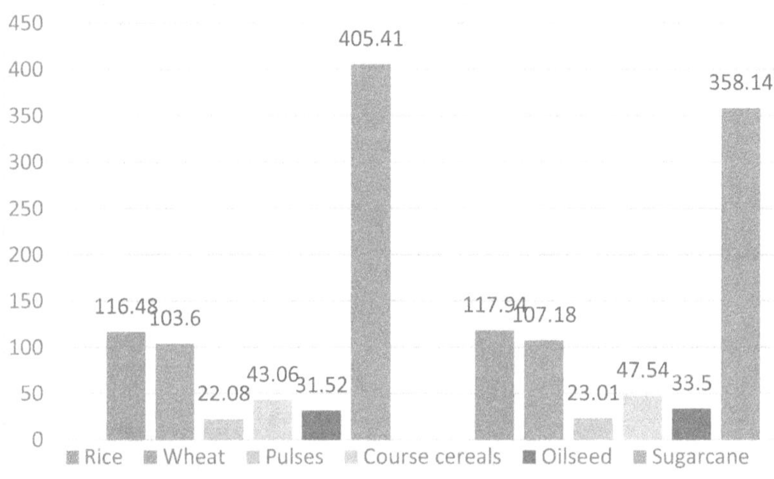

Source: agriculture ministry, figs: in million tonnes

The bars are represented from left to right as rice, wheat, pulses, course cereals, oilseed, sugarcane for India. Comparison (Apr-Feb period) is made between 2019-20 with 2018-19.

Production of rice and wheat is a record showing robustness of our agricultural system. Cotton production is estimated to be about 8.01 million bales more than last year to record an estimate of 36.05 million bales (170 kilograms each). Production of sugarcane has dipped due to heavy rain in the states of Karnataka and Maharashtra.

Deforestation

More the forests are cut away, more would be the animal-human conflict. More would be the drawing nearer between animal-human beings. This might mean more virus transmission than ever imagined.

Some noted scientists say that "it is a matter of common sense to limit interaction between humans and wildlife, especially primates.

Feeding primates should be discouraged, regardless of the pandemic, in order to prevent not just the spread of the disease but also to minimize problematic human-primate interaction.

Nature- Land, rivers and forests

We will learn to live with insects and birds and nature and not disturb them for our safety. We may start living a happy life without buying as much.

The unfolding climate crisis, with the catastrophes that loom ahead, might pose a bigger challenge than covid-19, for humanity.

It has been said, "Momentous events tend to make people realize how fragile life is."

Possibly Covid-19 outbreak and this long period of isolation can teach us the art of forming deeper and more meaningful relationships, then that would be a silver lining in these dark and despairing times.

Places of Worship

Mosques, Churches, Gurudwaras and Temples

Technology can be effectively used to reduce mass gathering in churches, mosques, temples and gurudwaras, if priests live stream their daily prayers. Prayers and Sunday mass has become a virtual reality. Iftar parties have become virtual too. Churches have got Sunday mass on You Tube. Churches have created channels whereby one can listen to recording by priests. The means to communicate are the WhatsApp groups. This takes the devotees with a feeling closer to God.

Real estate

Few real estate agents have started interacting in a novel way of using technology with drones to provide a virtual tour of properties to connect builders, developers with buyers and tenants looking for value deals. Landlords, on the other hand with their tenants vacating to go back home are eager to have replacements. Lockdown conditions had made matters worse for both sides.

A real estate intermediary cum fund manager in India-Smart Owner, made few observations in their report sent to their clients, some of which is referred to below.

Pandemic and its impact on real estate sector

The intermediary views two "distinct possibilities: (a) the optimistic scenario would be that the steps being taken quickly bring the outbreak under control, with no medium-term damage to the economy, and (b) the pessimistic scenario would be that the outbreak is not brought completely under control, but a substantially flattened curve permits the resumption of economic activity but with certain adjustments until a vaccine or cure is found."

They further add that under the optimistic scenario, material impact of the Covid-19 outbreak on the real estate sector may be minimal except that it may to some extent accelerate the adoption of online shopping at the expense of high street stores. This could strengthen warehousing and logistics assets at the expense of retail and malls.

In a pessimistic scenario, there may be a more nuanced impact on the sector and different sub-segments within the sector would have very different outlooks as given under.

A. Hospitality
It is possible that this segment could be most adversely affected by a prolonged period due to pandemic outbreak safeguards. MICE (Meetings, Incentives, Conferences, Exhibitions) may take longer than usual to come back soon. Levels of occupancy may remain depressed until the travel sector picks up. Weakness could continue for a few quarters and some good distressed assets could become available after a few quarters.

B. Retail
Physical retail may experience a prolonged slowdown lasting up to 3 or 4 quarters. With decreased footfalls in stores due to social distancing concerns, multiplexes may take longer time to come back to normalcy. It is possible that the downturn in retail may be offset, to some extent, by an increase in demand for warehouse and logistic assets.

C. Offices

Employers may to try to reduce the density of their people in workplaces to ensure the smooth operations of their business and also in response to the expectations of offshore clients. Working from home can lead to decreased productivity of employees and may not be a satisfactory solution. The ideal response would be to have more square footage of office space per employee. In the short run, the intermediary sees increased demand for managed office spaces and, in the medium-term, an increased demand for Grade A office spaces.

Office space: more space per person

While existing offices cannot be expanded, efficient planning and designing will offer a way out. Negotiations for new office spaces are expected to factor in revised space requirements.

Office (space per person) densification

Average densification will go back to the levels of 120-130 square feet as seen a decade back. Desk to desk spaces of 5.5 feet * 2.5 feet is good enough but social engagement spaces will have to be kept increased.

Companies are most likely to decide in using batches of employees and allowing 30% of the employees to work from home to work by rotation. This will result in lower occupation in offices and more space for all. It is unlikely to be a one-size -fits- all scenario.

D. Residential

Population growth, household income and demand drives the price in this segment. Irrespective of whether one is a landlord or a tenant, home becomes a necessity. Overall economic situation of a city determines the sustainability of residential prices. Possibly, a quarter will pass by before site visits by buyers can become a reality. Buyers will also be oriented to budget buys and affordable homes instead of splurging. The current scenario is in a way identical to the period soon after introduction of RERA (Real Estate Regulatory Authority). Unsold inventory is huge and they may come for bargain sales which can be utilized. The recovery will be faster within few quarters as home is an essential need and cannot be postponed for long unless possibility of future income of buyers gets disrupted.

With migrant laborers and workforce willing to operate from home, it may not be a farfetched reality for oneself to go back to their hometowns or nearer to their natives as they will be more satisfied to fend for themselves, meet their folks more often by spending less and even operating from their native towns and cities. This will bring down the tenancy in major cities. This shall also pave the way for recreation of a "NEW INDIA" with smaller mofussil towns and centers becoming cleaner, affordable with the best make-in facilities thus bringing down salaries and wages which in turn will add more unsold / unoccupied inventory of rented homes.

After all, why should everyone go for greener pastures to Delhi/ Bombay / Bangalore / Chennai in search of a better livelihood when one will have the freedom to operate from their own home which locale one is better adjusted to from childhood.

E. Commercial

Offices with large workforce may find it convenient to redefine their ways and means of working. Traffic snarls will be reduced. Chances are that officers and executives will find it easier to work from home unless connectivity, confidentiality and other service conditions force them to go to their respective offices.

If the table space distance is to be maintained, lesser staff will be required to work on shifts but for longer hours. Staggered lunch and break timings with no self-service in canteens could be the new cafeterias in workplaces.

Many companies have more than 3-5 office complexes in various parts of a city. It may possibly be a new way of defining their working by consolidating their operations in one or two spaces only thus making the others redundant.

Commercial complexes

Catering to wellness, health and safety requirement of employees after the Covid-19 outbreak are likely to push the operational expenditures of commercial complexes by at least 20%.

The new protocol would encompass several measures related to health and safety for all facility management teams, security protocols, thermal scanners, deep sanitization of common areas.

The business park owners in consultation with their global tenant may decide to have multiple measures such as screening at entrance to reduce risk of infected people coming in, more common areas, larger office spaces to ensure social distancing, availability of sanitizers and personal protective equipment.

Cafeterias and break out zones would have new layouts to prevent larger congregations, redesign and fit out new areas and use technology to track people better.

Real estate prices for IT (Information Technology) offices employing 4.3 million employees may come down. The overall occupancy of commercial space in the two southern cities of Bangalore and Hyderabad are 13 million sq. ft. and 11 million sq. ft. respectively.

Developers and landlords may show flexibility to acquire customers and is evidenced from the fact that India's largest IT employer TCS (Tata Consultancy Services) has announced that 3/4ths of its nearly 5 lakh employees would work remotely by 2025. The company spends Rs.6000.crs per year on real estate. ICIC Bank spends Rs.1200.crs per year on real estate. The larger effect of this whittling down remains to be seen.

Offices:

All employees can expect the following in their offices spaces:

- Too many people gathering at a conference room will be viewed as counterproductive
- Employees may dial in from different locations from the same office/ floor
- Doors that open automatically with sensors may become a norm
- Temperature may get recorded at different times of the day
- Hand sanitisers without pressing manually may be seen in rest rooms
- Notices sensitising employees to wash hands more regularly will be on display to remind one very often
- Sharing of phones or computers will be discouraged
- Employees may be provided with mask to be worn at work
- Work time and days may be staggered with longer shifts at work
- Common areas will be sanitised periodically
- Rest rooms will ensure plumbing is up to the mark
- Toilets (with lids)/ Employee ratio may become a norm

Warehousing:

A draft National logistics policy stated that logistics cost in our country is estimated at 13-14% of GDP as compared to 9-11% of GDP in the US and Europe and Japan. Warehousing sector allows 100% FDI and that is an attractive proposition.

India's warehouses were concrete in nature but it requires modernization with air conditioning, robotics and automation and a horizontal space in an affordable land.

With a possible manufacturing shift out of India and e-commerce expected to rule the roost, post Covid-19, players in India in the warehousing segment have been Hiranandani, Embassy group, Indo Space, Welspun, etc. Most of these groups are backed by Private Equity firms. For e-commerce companies and with a single country GST norm, if a firm cannot store enough and build a buffer of goods, it cannot meet the demand and neither can it deliver fast.

Many e-commerce companies are expected to boom, as people make a behavioral shift from buying offline to shopping online.

Across 8 Indian cities, NCR, Mumbai, Bengaluru, Pune, Kolkata, Chennai, Hyderabad, Ahmedabad- quality warehousing stock totaled 211 million sq. ft. in 2019. The stock is expected to rise to 253 million sq. ft. and would in most probability reach 300 million sq. ft. in 2021, as per JLL, a real estate services firm.

The WFH (Work from Home) may result in resource shift to smaller towns. If employees can get placed in Tier-2 cities, it would increase local consumption of daily requirements and hence the need for warehousing and supply chain companies to set up their base in these locations as cost considerations may work favorably too.

For a sustainable logistics supply chain model, the government needs to open up its thoughts and get into a joint venture / PPP (Public Private Partnership) model so as to get a better deal between the owners of the land belonging to the private sector, the Indian Railways (for the land running alongside the railway track lines) and the Government across most cities and towns.

CHAPTER-3

LABOUR

Cloud kitchen

This is a new found concept where kitchens will work round the clock with takeaway dining. The concept has taken big time as an internet driven food and beverage outfit supplying to orders by cooking for customers with the help of staff.

Here, kitchen, work areas are sanitized. Staff undergo temperature screening and packaging is given due respect before handing over to the riders for delivery to pre–paid orders received from customers.

Corporates

It is possible that corporates will try to diversify their chains across regions and geographies so that their operations are disruption free in another part of the world. With pandemics having proven its deep unpredictability, JIT(Just-In-Time) system would require exact demand forecasts for it to revert to its original exalted status. Many public listed companies will stop providing quarter to quarter guidance to stay relevant as demand and supply forecasting has become increasingly difficult.

Several captive companies/ centers of global companies in view of the ongoing crisis may be put up for sale or shutdown. There are about 1400 captives in India and about 1700 in the Philippines and broader Asia Pacific Region. About 40% of all the captives have under 500 employees. Monetization of these centers to improve operations and adding cash infusions to the clients may become the order of the day.

Issues with data processing norms, imposed by regulators, could also result in work moving back onshore, but the repatriation of the work would likely be for the short term.

Clubs- are generally run for members by the members administered by an elected committee of office bearers.

At clubs, sanitizers will greet you at the reception entry. Tables in restaurants will be separated far and wide and contactless dining without menu card will be the order of the day. Many a curbs will keep socializing a distant reality.

Innovation

How do you stay calm and innovate in a crisis?

How do you stay focused on what you can do and not worry about what is beyond your control?

Most innovation as per T. N. Hari, co-author of Saying No to Jugaad: The Making of Big Basket, is all about little changes about thinking creatively and out of the box. As per him, a crisis can trigger innovation and can bring out the best in some individuals. Think clearly and act decisively. Question, conventional wisdom.

In a difficult period like the pandemic, Reliance-Jio-Facebook-WhatsApp deal is an innovation and is a masterstroke and a matter to cheer about as an Indian.

Jobs

Emphasis on Government jobs

People in Government jobs come unscathed, post the Covid-19.

Few sacrifices, here and there, but job security which is paramount in ones' lifetime gets attained here with a Government job. In times like these, it is also the most power wielding position that matters. Be it a health inspector or a police inspector, all have come out to be feared as they had the rule book in their hand.

Private sector jobs

Post the Covid-19 lockdown, young and energetic workforce will find themselves to be at a disadvantage as they will be working on shifts from longer working hours. Few of the Sundays may be a working day for many like the call center executives who practice their principals' workload offshored to India, for example a call center servicing a credit card of a large bank. In India, unlike their western counterparts, taking work home and attending to them even on weekends is a norm by itself.

Job market

Huge demand is likely to erupt in e- commerce companies. People at the lower end of the job market, if laid off have a huge opportunity in these e-commerce companies. Amazon, for instance is creating 50,000 new temporary jobs in India.

The current pandemic outweighs the previous crises because of the number of industries hurt and the countries it has swamped.

The outbreak of the virus is likely to make companies seek more gig workers than hire employees with a fixed salary.

White collar jobs

Every company has clamped down on new hiring to keeping expenses low. There is complete freeze in sectors like aviation, tourism, hospitality, e-commerce, media, logistics, real estate, construction, etc.

Most companies have scrapped performance appraisals towards performance cum variable bonus and have sent employees on leave without pay. Companies with lower cash flows have retrenched some staff.

Post Covid-19, the variable pay might go above 50% (earlier 40%) for VP's and above and at mid management roles it might become 30-40% (up from 15-20%)

Junior roles which may not have had variable pay will include 5-10% to recognize the concept all across the organization.

The CMIE (Centre for Monitoring Indian Economy) has stated that the count of salaried employees some of whom could be blue collared has dropped from 86 million in 2019-20 to 68 million in April'2020.

Recruitment and Staffing firms

With increased layoffs and retrenchments and salary cuts, loyalty will be the last most important factor in the minds of an employee. With higher uncertainty, one may start working towards a more stable job by even relinquishing their current employment. Higher perks and promises of the future may be kissed a good bye. This would be more visible with youngsters below 30. Graduates between 25-30 may start applying for Government / Semi Government jobs. The lure of joining start-ups may be kept on the backburner for some time to come.

Finance, tech and consumer goods firms will be the flavor for recruitment and job switches. Lifestyle changes during lockdown will also drive demand for financial consultants, factory workers, animators, delivery workers. As months pass by, demand for skilled and competency based job roles will go up.

Retrenched employees have to quickly relearn and also utilize the time to get certified with new online courses and get upgraded for a newer role or activity and be available in the recruitment space to get absorbed and show multi- dimensional skills.

Younger professionals can adapt to this change while the older and experienced persons in the higher age and income brackets will lose out and may get displaced. This is the time lead for oneself to newer opportunities and possibilities.

Self- employed (skilled, semi-skilled and unskilled) and professionals

Plumbers, electricians, masons are self-employed people. Lawyers, chartered accountants, architects, construction engineers, surveyors possibly fall under this category.

In view of the financial year end, many Chartered Accountants have started doing auditing and vouching (verifying the vouchers and ticking them that they have perused) vide online means. It is a completely new exercise. During formative years, in CA article ship (read-internship) usually for 3 years, the fun is in using the green and red ink than the blue ink as the fun is in highlighting to the senior auditor of the mistakes that one has found out by highlighting. Never would this become evident anymore. Possibly in the audit report made over a MS word file, the analysis has to be highlighted in the said color ink.

Lawyers generally are lined up outside court rooms to dwell on their matters arguing with their counterparts when called upon to do so by their judges on the appointed days. The court hall is generally full.

Now they have to follow norms of physical distancing and possibly most of the arguments could be conducted online. However, the decorum of the courts should be maintained even when arguments are sought from ones' home by wearing the advocates attire and the my- lords have to be respected and one continues to stand as it would now get recorded which is a good evidence for the time to come. Possibly this will hasten up the hearings of many cases as courts could be open on any day as per the convenience of the judges and the opposing cum consenting parties. This would in turn mean that in rural towns, virtual court sessions could become the order of the day. Imagine, a farmer with connectivity and joining a court room hearing, sitting at his hometown instead of travelling to the local municipal headquarters and losing sleep to attend to a hearing. A good development indeed!

Staff welfare-equipment

The coffee / tea vending machines on display replacing the coffee / tea supplier of the past may become much less useful in offices.

Teachers

Teachers would play a significant part in grooming the young and the old. Both in schools and colleges teachers have a role in making the children and the young adolescents to keep distance between themselves and also with the teachers.

- How would one punish a boy / girl?
- How would one monitor tests and examinations?

The school headmaster and headmistress and the principals have a humungous responsibility of using sanitizers, reduce friction between human beings and have the lowest interaction when in the school premises.

Playgrounds, toilets, corridors require constant mopping and cleaning, else the licenses of many schools could be withdrawn.

Women's livelihoods

The ILO (International Labor Organization) estimates that nearly 200 million jobs will be lost in the next few months alone in small scale services like hairdressing, domestic workers, street vendors, causal laborers, etc. especially dominated by women who carry the weight of their extended families.

Just as women lose jobs in these segments there could be increased demand in old age homes, maintenance of schools under close down, overwhelmed health systems, etc.

With schools remaining closed, women may have to fend their children while trying to maintain a balance between household and their employment.

The inequality is evident with 70% healthcare workers being women and are easily outnumbered by men in healthcare management and comprise of 10% in the political sphere.

Women in insecure jobs need basic social protections, from health insurance to paid sick leave, childcare and unemployment benefits. Increasingly, the Governments of the world should start focusing on better support system like cash transfers, loans and bailouts, credit, etc.

Women professionals

With W-F-H set to become a norm, for a large section of the workforce, several companies will be opening a plethora of opportunities targeting women looking to make a comeback. Women who are giving a second shot at their career, post childbirth, etc. may get a chance. However, they need to be flexible, keeping learning online and develop their skills to go beyond.

W-F-H will no longer come in the way of career progression, promotions and pay increases. Women may have to get into the drivers' seat to promote themselves aggressively.

E-commerce companies will look at customer service roles and rekindling desire for purchase of products.

Workers' rights

As published in a local newspaper[5], "The Labor Ministry issued an advisory on March 20'2020 requesting (a.) companies to continue to pay wages to employees during the lockdown period and (b.) private/ public enterprises to not terminate employees or reduce their wages and to consider employees on leave as deemed to be on duty without wage deduction."

On March 29'2020, the Ministry of Home Affairs issued an order under the Disaster Management Act'2005, directing that during the lockdown period, employers shall make wage payments on the due date without any deductions.

On April 27'2020, in response to a batch of writ petitions challenging validity of the order, a 3 bench judge of the Supreme Court directed

---

[5] Sriram Bhavya, Arvind, Article, The Hindu, Business Line, 02/05/2020

the Centre to 'place its polity' on record.

Many companies have paid while some have taken different stances to compensate employees and workers. Retrenchment, lay-offs, etc. as defined by various laws (Industrial Disputes Act'1947) may require a re-look and an amendment in light of the recent pandemic. Companies employing workers will have their own story to tell.

Few States in India like UP, MP and Gujarat have used the lockdown period to suspend labor laws on prescribed minimum wages act'1948, Industrial Disputes Act'1947, Industrial Relations Code'2019 allowing third party inspection of factories through what is called inspector-cum-facilitator, etc., The suspension of the labor laws range from 1000 days (MP state) to 3 years (UP state). Possibly, the State Governments are trying to project themselves as investor-friendly. For an economy caught in a downward spiral, will these changes to labor rights stimulate private investment and economic recovery, only time will tell.

Working in manufacturing organizations and on shop floors

When workers report to work, they have to undergo few tests and provide a declaration of their health and their family members. They may have to walk through a sanitizing tunnel. They would not be allowed to share their tools and they would have to maintain safe distance with their colleagues else their wristband would vibrate.

The shop floors will have to recalibrate their assembly lines to undertake safety and health protocols.

Large companies are building demarcated work areas on shop floors with plastic screen shields, re-laid assembly lines, automating and digitizing various processes to reduce human interaction, working with 50% manpower and more shifts, sanitizing tunnel of disinfectant mist of sodium hydrochloride for workers, big trucks and vehicles, PPE for security staff, continuous monitoring of employee health, and automated sanitizer dispensers.

Further, there will be a gap of one hour between one shift and another so as to get the sanitizing of all spaces done. This is akin to airlines getting cleaned up between arrival and departure of one sector. Tools will be coded and identified so that each person has a dedicated tool. Non touch based washing system may be introduced in select factories.

All these have an investment built into it and with staff at 50% of the capacity, unless the demand picks up the immediate benefit is ruled out.

Even raw materials upon purchase shall be going through an incubation period before going to the shop floor.

Quality control and quality assurance will have lower set of employees and with limited batch strength. "There is a case to move from efficiency based approach to include efficacy elements in the post Covid-19 production principles and practices" - Vinay Raghunath, auto practice head at Ernst Young, as quoted in a newspaper.

Apprenticeship programs will restart to include new courses to cater to the needs of MNC's (Multi-National Companies) that may be relocating their manufacturing to India. This would enable our apprenticeship programs to be at par with the US and EU countries. In India, less than 0.1% of the employed workforce or just 0.3 million people are apprentices. In comparison, the UK has 1.5% or 0.5 million. China has 2.5% or 20 million. Germany has 5% or 2.5 million apprentices.

India's current apprenticeship scheme allows 15% of an organizations total workforce to be apprentices and firms with 30 or more number of employees will have to mandatorily hire apprentices.

CHAPTER- 4

CAPITAL

Advertising industry

Covid-19 has brought the advertising industry into a difficult situation. Most of the commitments made in Jan and Feb'20 is getting fulfilled. However, come May'20, decline in advertising agencies is expected. While news channels are least hit, entertainment channels saw a 34% decline and film channels a 43% decline in advertising.

Only a few brands in the essential category, such as hand washes and soaps and social messaging around coronavirus, online education and insurance firms are on air.

For the first time, Reckitt Benckiser has overtaken Hindustan Unilever in marketing spends during this period.

Not only are the ad inventories running low, ad rates have also slumped. With TV viewership being high, possibly advertisers are missing out on a golden opportunity to make their mark. Those having foresight and money to advertise will benefit by getting a much bigger share of viewers' attention.

Aviation

The new rules of flying as furnished in Appendix-1 with the Standard Operating Procedures(SOP's) can make one believe that s/he is travelling to Mars, considering the PPE and other safeguards being taken by the cabin crew and the passengers. This is the first time in aviation history that aircrafts and crew are getting back into service after 2 months of halt. This, in turn, would require special care and caution as the entire system has to be re-accustomed to the endless routine checklists and procedures.

Daily losses have been soaring for the aviation sector with no respite in sight. The Government has announced plans to privatize more airports, free up more airspace for civilian flights, cut taxes to make India an attractive center for MRO (Maintenance and Repair Operations) of aircraft. Few countries have helped airlines in the form of soft loans of undoing in exchange of a minority stake in the airline, as per Ameya Joshi, founder of Network Thoughts.

The sector has been seeking deferment of GST, bringing jet fuel under GST, reduction in airport charges and overflight fees, taxing passengers on security, temporary reduction of excise duty on jet fuel. Aviation turbine fuel have fallen over 65% amidst the global drop in crude prices. The revenue loss is estimated to be 11.2 billion USD this year, putting 2.9 million jobs at risk as passenger demand has fallen by over 47%.

As per E&Y India, Indian airlines, have all borrowings in forex (by way of foreign aircraft leases or foreign Exim backed loans) and have little collateral to offer for new loans as most aircraft's are not owned by them but mortgaged and have a negative working capital so to raise unsecured debt from the banking system can be a Herculean challenge.

The aviation sector also has airport firms, ground handling firms, airport retailers which form an important support to the sector. They are expected to post losses of 3-3.6. billion in USD in the quarter, according to CAPA India. Unless promoters of the aviation companies are able to capitalize the downsizing of the sector could become inevitable.

Automobiles

The stimulus did not provide demand kicker for the auto industry. The suppliers to larger OEM's also feel the pinch as wages and salaries is the bigger element of cost after raw materials. With only loans as the breather and not direct cash subsidy or reduction in GST and an incentive-based scrap page policy, the industry's supply chains could be impacted further. For the first time in the history of India's largest four-wheeler manufacturing company, Maruti, the sales were "zero" in April'2020. The trend for the future months could be disappointing across the sector.

Brands

In a published newspaper interview[6] it has been said that "the world may not be the same again. The rules of business will change. Brands that can use this opportunity to build a world that is more compassionate, connected, experiential and meaningful will emerge stronger on the other side."

Companies and their plans

Covid-19 has helped many companies to start looking at innovative products, services and have thereby increased their product range by diversifying or expanding. Vertical integration has emerged in some cases. From a perfumery plant, which is not a necessity in today's times, a company has started manufacturing sanitizers instead. Some from printing technology have ventured to distribute Covid-19 related products like thermometers, masks, sanitizers, etc. to name a few. These are glaring examples of how promoters think of making their cash registers ringing and ensuring footfalls in their shops.

---

[6] Gurtaney.Navin, Article, Mint

These are encashment of business opportunities by utilizing idle capacities.

Every company / firm will keep more than 2 contingency plans; Plan A and Plan B to drive businesses forward. Plan A is for the first 3 months and Plan B is for a contingency extending well beyond a decade.

Typically, these can be called as long-term contingency plans and with a diversification and risk mitigation in mind.

Many companies and their Boards and their auditors will now find it difficult to assess and certify the going concern status of businesses as the liquidity situation is precarious and is likely to deteriorate further with lower demand for their goods and services.

This is particularly important as per accounting standard Ind-AS1 as it mandates that financial statements can be prepared as a going concern only if the management has no plans to liquidate the company or has realistic alternatives to such a prospect. The managements outlook of its business and especially on material uncertainties that cast doubts about the survival of the company, these should be disclosed.

With uncertainty around how the pandemic evolves, businesses have to assess if the worth of their non-financial assets, including plant and machinery has eroded.

Electric Vehicles (EV)

Electric vehicles came to the fore to overcome worries on climate changes. With healthcare and stimulus gaining steam, will the old objectives with long term implications be given a go by?

In Europe, despite the austerity measures, Governments are keen to reduce the carbon footprint. As per Dr V. Sumatran, author of 'Faster, Smarter, Greener: the Future of the Car and Urban Mobility, in his newspaper article[7] says that "a broad spectrum of reforms and investments are aimed at urban rejuvenation, renewable energy, tougher emission standards, investing in EV Charging infrastructure."

As per Dr Sumatran, there are sound business reasons for electrification as the cost of renewable energy has dropped to a point where it will remain viable under reasonable long-term forecasts of crude-oil prices.

IBC (Insolvency and Bankruptcy Code) proceedings

With the economy in disarray for the next 6-10 quarters, bidders of insolvent companies may back off as their own prospects are affected. Fighting for ones' own survival is key rather than acquiring companies.

Bankers may face a double whammy of forcing to sell an asset below the liquidation value.

Promoters who were barred from negotiating may get a nod-in as the bidder may back off. This view is exactly opposite of what the IBBI (Insolvency and Bankruptcy Board of India) had suggested few months back. Possibly more foreign suitors may have to be made to step up rather than depend upon domestic buyers as foreign investors may have higher liquidity.

---

[7] Sumantran. V, Article, The Hindu-Business Line, 09/05/20

There could be a pause in the rules governing bankruptcies and business acquisitions around the world. Hard times have befallen most companies; the difference is relative. If weak businesses have to be taken over by the bigger ones, anti-monopoly laws have to be eased. Many companies looking for intellectual property, human resources, distribution networks from the small scale ones could find right suitors in big companies. A round of buy-outs would also save jobs.

Industries impacted in India and its tail

Based on a study by few Industry Associations in India, Figure-5 is furnished with the time taken to recover in select industries as a consequence to the lockdown.

Figure 5- Time lag of select industries to bounce back in India, post Covid-19

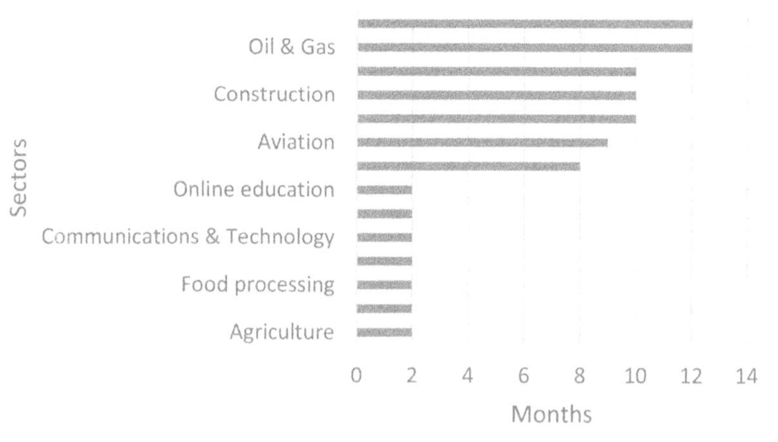

The longest time to recovery will in all likelihood be in oil & gas, construction, aviation of over 8 months.

Investments in Equity stocks and Companies

Despite having the highest cash in their books, Charlie Munger and Warren Buffett are quietly sitting on their cash holdings of 125 USD billions (Rs.10. lakh crores). They believe that this is a situation on which no one seems to know what is unfolding. As Charlie Munger says: "This thing is different. Everybody talks as if they know what is going to happen, and nobody knows what is going to happen."

The drivers for equity investments in companies shall possibly in the new normal be the following for a high-ticket investor:

1. Non-discretionary consumption growth offering visibility- Companies that have better technology leveraging ability – ed-tech, healthcare, logistics, etc.
2. Well capitalised businesses- Companies which have higher liquidity and solvency.
3. Ability pay dividends – When growth is difficult investors try to grapple with dividend yielding stocks.
4. Agility in forging deals
5. Short term is the new Long term – investment style is likely to be for short term active trading instead of long-term passive investing. Besides companies per se, various internal and external factors are adding to the volatility.

Fear, Greed and Hope

By examining 3 different days in 2020, Feb 28th, March 23rd and May 15th, the concept of fear, greed and hope can be explained in Figure-6.

On Feb 28th, we lived with **greed** as the market expectation was favorable, post the crash of the equity index on March 23rd, we started living on **fear** and started hoping for the worst and on May 15th, with some consolidation, we have started **hoping** to get back to the Feb 28th levels and to the historic highs of the past.

All of these ups and downs are virtuous cycle which play out as an investors emotion and his corresponding behavior.

Figure 6- Movement of India's Nifty Index on 3 days during 2020

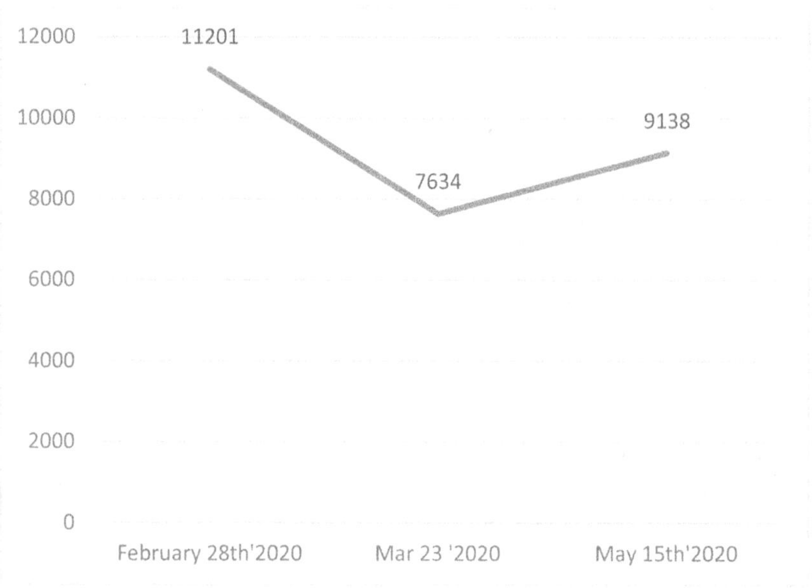

Source: NSE India

MSCI India Index (INR)

The MSCI India Index designed to measure the performance of the large and midcap segments of the Indian market. With 84 constituents, the index covers approximately 85% of the Indian equity universe.

Figure-7 portrays the cumulative index performance- in gross returns in INR for the period April'2005- April'2020.

Figure 7- Cumulative annual comparison (INR) of MSCI EM vs MSCI India vs MSCI BRIC (%)

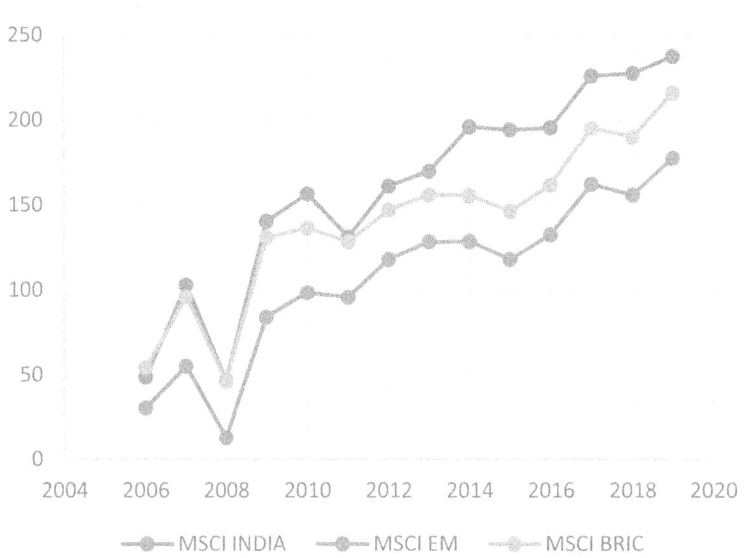

Source: MSCI.com

When read from the bottom line to the top line, in Figure-7 the following is the order:

- MSCI Emerging Markets
- MSCI BRIC
- MSCI India

In Figure-8, performance of investment returns (in %) is presented across asset classes. The bars are represented from left to right in the orders of sensex (equity index), gold, cash, fixed deposit across the time periods of 1 week, 1 year, 3 years and 5 years.

Figure-8 depicts, major underperformance in India across financial asset classes due to coronavirus.

Figure 8- Investment Returns across asset class over varying time horizons

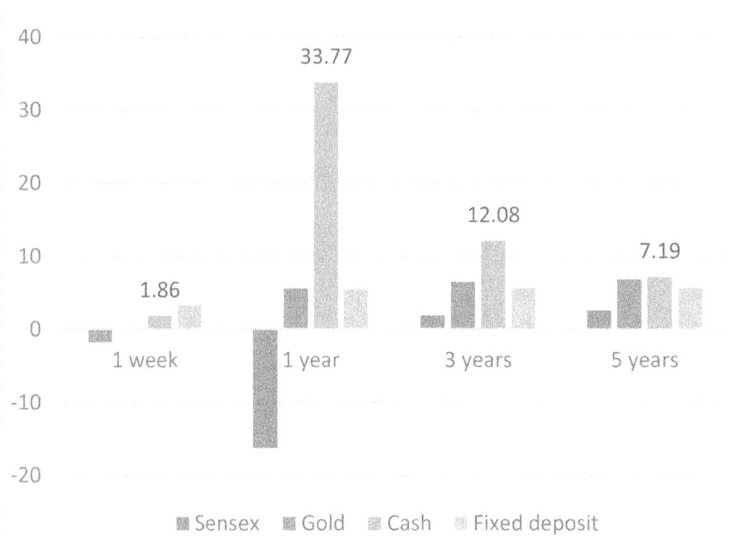

Source: SBI, Bloomberg, Value Research as on 15/05/2020

Lending

A disruption like this pandemic will have many implications in shaping our economic and financial behavior and responses for few years. Much of them will be beneficial for increasing our operational efficiencies. One of the significant changes will be acceleration in the already ongoing shift to digital channels for conducting everyday business. Banks and financial intermediaries, in collaboration with the fintech ecosystem and enabled by GOI (Government of India) digitization initiatives, will be further empowered to extend formal access to credit and other financial services to hitherto unfunded segments of the economy.

NPA's (Non-Performing Assets) are expected to rise sharply, post the moratorium period, both on the retail and corporate loans as insolvencies may rise unless Government steps in.

Loan borrowers

The large borrowers would have a way to service their loans or to seek waiver of penalties and moratoriums.

The salaried class will possibly borrow more to tide over their crisis. The prepayment or foreclosure would be an option seldom used by many.

The low-ticket borrowers not knowing how to fend for themselves may even go into hiding. These are generally the personal loan / credit card/ 2 wheeler borrowers.

The digital loan providers possibly may be running out of capital and will be choosy, not willing to let go their loans so easily as made out to be.

NBFC's (Non-Banking Finance Companies) are keen to maintain their credit rating and will be more eager to maintain their repayment status with loan lending as the last priority. Those who would have lent loans based on algorithmic lending will face a host of issues.

Microfinance companies who have lent in the rural hinterland will also face delinquency however supportive their digital payment systems are. Livelihoods in rural areas need to get back but the possibility of the farming community coming back to terms will be faster than their urban counterparts.

Seekers of gold loan takers will be high as traders and shopkeepers who do not have access to formal financing will fund their existence through this route for some time and will continue to grow.

Private Equity (PE) funds

While exit timelines will get delayed, there is bound to be sharp drop in value of investments. This has forced many PE companies to receive margin calls on loans availed by them against the portfolio of their shares.

The portfolio value of almost all PE funds might get to slash their returns by 15-20% which means that the return for the last year could be a washout.

We might see lot more PIPE (Private Investment in Public Equity) transactions by volume, not value as compared to previous year as many of these assets are available at relatively attractive valuations.

Micro, Small Medium Enterprises (MSME's)

The MSME sector contributes 30.3% to India's GDP in FY 19. The UK Sinha panel estimates the overall supply of finance from formal sources to MSME's at Rs.14.5. trillion and the credit gap at Rs.20-25. trillion.

The sources for tables-3,4,5 are as under:

- Report of the expert committee on MSME, June 2019;
- NIPFP paper titled Savings and Capital formation in India by Ila Patnaik and Radhika Pandey, June'2019;
- 2017 NSSO titled key indicators of unincorporated non-agricultural enterprises (excluding construction) in India.

Table 3- Comparison of MSME's outstanding bank credit (%)

Industry	2017-18	2013-14
MSME's	6.3	8.5
Large corporates	28.9	37.0
Services	26.7	24.2
Retail loans	24.8	18.3
Agriculture and allied activities	13.4	12.0

Table 4- State wise classification of MSME's in India (in million)

States	MSME's (In million)
Madhya Pradesh	2.7
Rajasthan	2.7
Gujarat	3.3
Andhra Pradesh	3.4
Bihar	3.4
Karnataka	3.8
Maharashtra	4.8
Tamil Nadu	4.9
West Bengal	8.9
Uttar Pradesh	9.0

Just 10 states account for three fourths of the 63.4 million MSME's in India.

MSME loans go bad (represented in % terms) due to payment delays (41) from customers, change in promoter holding (10), withdrawal of capital (10), other reasons (10), other competitive factors like changes in regulation or when faced with business loss (29).

Figure 9- Reasons why MSME loans go bad in India (%)

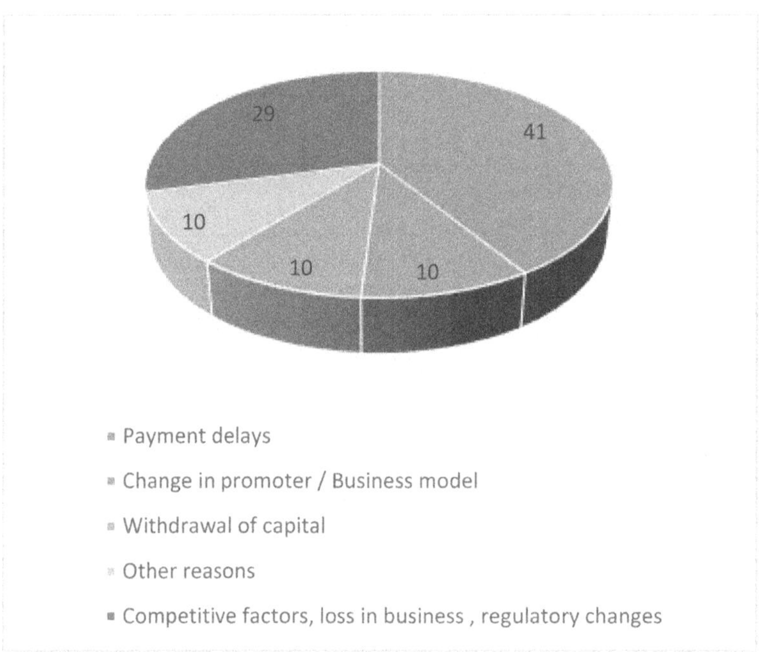

Table 5- Comparison of working capital and receivable cycles for MSME's in India during crisis periods of 2000,2010,2020

Year	Working capital cycle (days)	Debtors (days)
2020	450	220
2010	790	240
2000	350	120

The peak is yet to be attained as the cycle is just getting stretched with only 40 days of lockdown in force.

About 71% of MSME's failed to pay wages – fully or partially for March'20 according to a data from an industry body.

There is a crying need for help to this segment and a guarantee by government will allow risk averse banks to start lending. RBI's data shows total bank loans to small businesses standing at Rs.4.78. trillion as of Feb'20. Loans when guaranteed will go to facilitate only the registered MSME with GST records.

The US has announced $ 359 billion in forgivable small business administration loans and guarantee to help small business that retain workers as part of its $ 2 trillion Covid-19 package. In the UK, there is a talk of offering 100% government-guaranteed loans to small business to ensure these companies do not go into bankruptcy.

Protection of small businesses in US, UK and select European nations

Countries around the world in USA, UK, Europe have taken various measures to provide relief to small businesses as shown in Table-6.

It varies from (i.) provision of unsecured loans without evaluation of credit to SME's; (ii.) payment of utility bills on behalf of the companies; (iii.) payment of salaries and wages for a limited period; (iv.) participation with equity; (v.) freeze on rental payments for a limited period; (vi.) moratorium or deferral or reduction of taxes, etc. to name a few.

Table 6- Support provided by select countries to small businesses, post Covid-19

Countries	Support provided
France	Unsecured loans with 90% coverage, up to 5 million euro for SME's. "Rebound loans" without guarantee to up to 500000 euros. Government to pay rent, gas and electricity bills for small companies.
Germany	One time payments of up to 9000 euro for 3 months, for units with up to 5 employees. One time payments of up to 15000 euro with up to 10 employees. Euro 100 billion for direct equity participation in businesses.
Italy	4 billion euros' package to help SME's address cash flow needs and diversify into export markets. New loans for a maximum of 25000 euros for up to 6 years to SME's, freelancers without credit evaluation.
Spain	6 months' moratorium on taxes for SME's and self-employed. Freeze on rental payments for 2 months.
UK	6 months' interest free, Business Interruption Loan scheme raised from 1.2 million pounds to 5 million pounds. Bounce back loans between 2000-50000 pounds with no fees, interest to pay for first 12 months.
USA	Provided 50 billion USD loans + business interruption loans without interest of up to $ 10 million. Tax reductions and deferral for businesses of all sizes.

Source: Economic Times, 16/05/2020

Rent control Act amidst pandemic

There is a clarion call from tenants to landlords to forego rentals for one or two months as they are in distress. Government, civil society, academia, and migrants themselves are urging landlords to stop evictions as it would exacerbate the pandemic.

Generally, in our country most rental agreements are informal and unrecorded. Most requests to waive rent or stop evictions is on the basis of Disaster Management Act, 2005 which does not have the necessary provisions to maintain continuation of rental housing arrangements. This is better done when rent control acts is used.

The Rent controls of various states and the Central Governments Model Tenancy Act'2019 should overlap to help such uncertainties to be managed to everyone's satisfaction.

Landlords in our country are seen as capitalists. The truth on the other hand when it comes to retail/ housing rental landlords are different as the landlords themselves are over dependent on the monthly rental for their survival in majority of the cases. This is because the landlords are not covered by social security net and do not have much savings to fend for themselves.

Therefore, it is necessary that the rent control act should ensure that the landlords and tenants be known along with the details of the property and its location.

The Model Tenancy Act should in effect ensure that a portal be created for registration of rental agreements be established through State Governments and linked with the income Tax Act and to overcome rent collection in cash. This Act may also build in a 'Force Majeure' clause for emergencies like these.

So as to safeguard the landlords who may deprived of their rent, a separate fund be created by the Central Government, which can be partly funded while registering the agreements. Housing, welfare, disaster fund, it may be called.

This sort of arrangement will enable safety net for both landlords and the tenants alike.

Start ups

Start-up morale could be in lockdown. Despondency is taking hold of start-ups in India that are shrinking operations amid the lockdown, putting jobs on the line. Many newly funded start-ups have taken resignation letters from its employees within minutes across e-mails. For those retained, the salary cuts are sharper ranging between 50-70%. Many employees are being put on their bench.

Some (key employees) will retain jobs and resume, some will have to take pay cuts to retain their jobs and others may be fired. The irony is that many employees quit their better paying jobs to seek a new found enthusiasm. Will they be able to get back to their former employer is a question?

Start-ups will have to have free runway for 12-18 months and seek lower valuation before going public. It is possible that markets have to stabilize and allow winners to play out. Companies have to rejig their business models to stay relevant.

The start-ups have sought funding support from the Government and it may be unlikely that socialism of losses with privatization of profit may not be followed in this case. This is especially relevant as start-ups have been provided benefits like tax deferrals etc. for 3 years. All Start-ups cannot be equated on the same page as they are in different phases: early / nurtured / pre-IPO stage etc.

ACBC – (After Corona Before Corona)

In a published newspaper interview[8] the head of a PE firm, says that "at present, businesses need to focus on long term sustainability including business continuity and safeguarding employees. Besides conserving cash, advice includes revising the business plans, revisiting business assumptions, moderate expectations on timelines for fund raising and valuations, step up communications with customers, communicate with teams on the business strategy, maintain health and safety, strengthen Board and advisors with credible members who have managed business through multiple cycles, watch out for concentrations: by customers, vendors, geographies, etc.". It is expected that a combination of digital and offline business models will evolve where technology will augment delivery of products and services to NHB (Next Half Billion) Indians.

Driven by investor attempts to cut losses and save face, one can expect drop in valuations, spike in M&A's (Merger and Acquisitions) and distressed sales. The current crisis will in most likelihood lead to a large number of start- up failures, as deprived of capital, ill-conceived and collapsing business models, etc.

NASSCOM survey[9] of 9300 start-ups in India shows falling revenues of 92% respondents. While 62% have seen revenues dip by more than 40%, 34% have seen revenues plummet by over 80%. As per the survey analysis, the impact of the coronavirus is that 60% of B2C start-ups are facing closure while 40% of start- ups are temporarily shut or winding up operations. Only 8% have cash reserves for over 9 months while 22% have 3-6 months' cash to survive. Majority, about 70% of them have cash of 0-3 months.

---

[8] Kudva Roopa, Interview, Mint, 30/04/2020

[9] NASSCOM, survey Apr/May'2020, Mint

The internet start-ups were suffering even before the pandemic, as despite heavy spending, they were unable to make profits now with a slackening demand, problem will get accentuated. Soft bank with its vision fund invested 75 USD billion in 88 start ups and have reported losses of 18 billion USD.

Those start-ups who did not have the right business model but were running with the hope that they will figure a way out, will find the going tough as gaining finance is ruled out as they would have burnt cash during good time and now cannot hope that investors will not stick their neck out to save them further.

Funding data reflects a sharp slowdown. According to Tracxn, Indian start-ups have raised 3.3 billion USD this year. With mega funding rounds unlikely, the 15.7 billion USD raised in 2019 may become a distant reality.

Between 2016 and now, more than 14000 start-ups have shut shop. Over the last 2 months 250+ start-ups have got added to that number. This "dead pool" as termed by Tracxn - a data platform tracking start-ups believes shall go up.

India has had several start-ups who are in the rice to raise more capital. To name a few: Oyo, Swiggy, Zomato, Cure. Fit, Grofers, Flipkart, Phone Pe, Myntra, Redbus, Snap deal, Free charge, Citrus Pay, Ola, Policy Bazar, Byjus etc.

In most of the competitive sectors, there are duopolies. It can be a face-saving merger and acquisition for investors in many cases. In few cases the No 2 and 3 may join to compete with the No 1, especially where difference in market share between 1 and 2 is wide.

Football leagues, stadiums and revenue impact, during Covid-19[10]

The disruption to the current football season and next season threatens the profitability and even survival of some football clubs in Europe. Cancellation of leagues will exacerbate the loss. However, if matches are held in closed door stadiums the losses will be limited as only gate receipts shall be lost.

In the next few paragraphs, we have tried to analyze the popular fan base and fallout of the lockdown measures and how football leagues as played in some European countries and the UK, Ireland, etc. have been impacted who otherwise can influence high revenues from various sources, enabling them to boost net profit of their popular clubs, who can carry out transfers (buy / sell) high class players and help win coveted championships, year after year.

Football clubs have several sources of revenue with the 4 principal ones being Broadcast, Sponsorship, Commercial, Gate receipts. If football is played behind closed doors, it will unlock 3 of the 4 sources of revenue, though not in full.

The break-down for each revenue stream (represented in % terms) in European football league is Domestic broadcasting (37), Sponsorship (22), Gate receipts (15), Revenue from UEFA (10), Commercial (8) and Other sources (8).

Figure 10 demonstrate the revenues of 2017-18 of larger leagues with break up amongst various revenue streams of each country to be varying on its share of dependence.

---

[10] Mint, closed door options in football, what happens to football stadiums, Article, Mint,15/04/20, pg-2

Figure 10- Revenue break up in larger football leagues in Europe

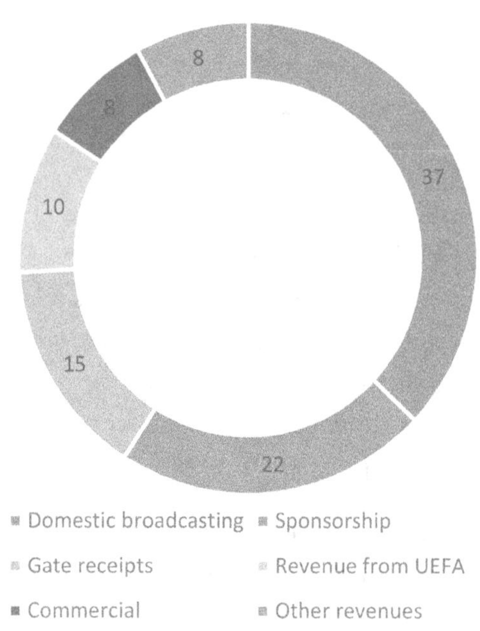

Source: UEFA Club licensing benchmarking report

Domestic broadcasting, sponsorship, gate receipts, revenue from UEFA account for 84% in European clubs as per Figure-10.

Larger football leagues have high domestic watchers followed by sponsorship in larger leagues.

Comparison of revenue between larger and smaller leagues is shown in Figures 11 and 12 respectively. From the Figure-12, it is found that Gate receipts are more critical for smaller leagues than larger ones.

Figure 11- Country-wise larger football league revenues (%) in Europe (2017-18)

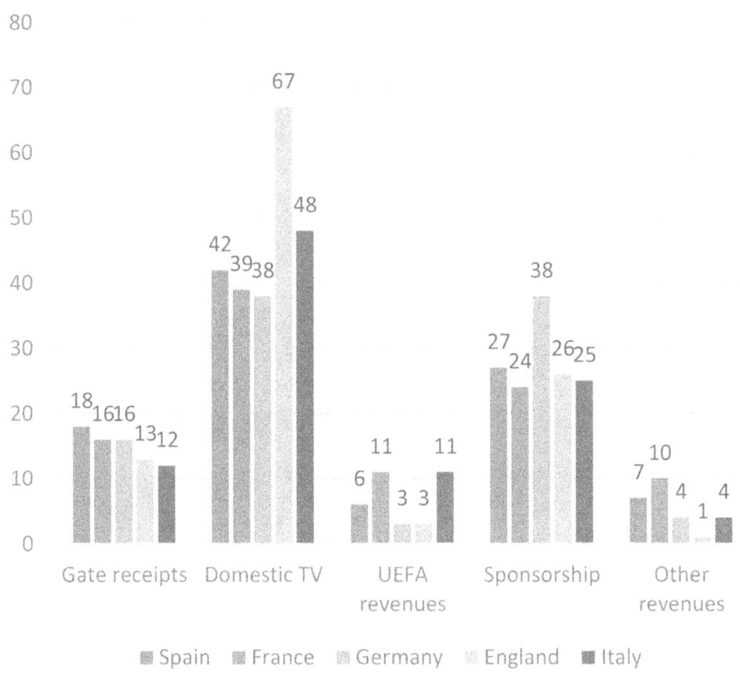

Source: UEFA Club licensing benchmarking report

When read, the bar charts against each revenue stream (represented in % terms) are arranged by country names in the following order:

- Spain
- France
- Germany
- England
- Italy

Figure 12- Country-wise smaller football league revenues (%) in Europe

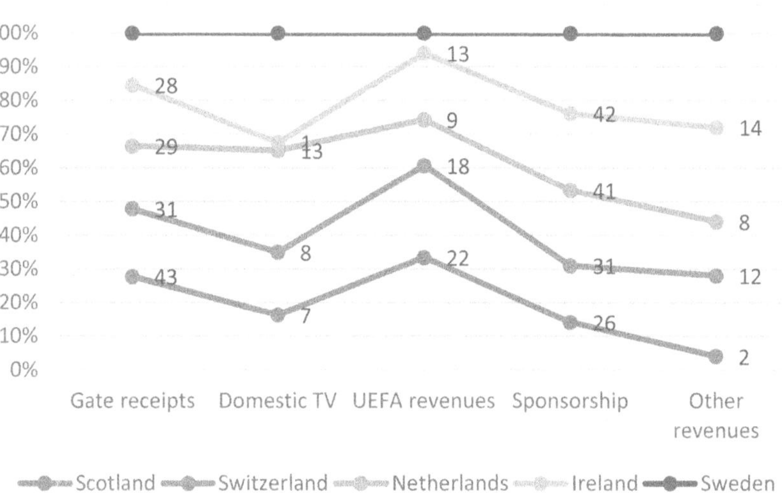

Source: UEFA Club licensing benchmarking report.

The lines in Figure-12 are represented by country names from top to bottom in the following order as below:

- Sweden

- Ireland

- Netherlands

- Switzerland

- Scotland

As per Figure-12, Smaller leagues clearly demonstrate the fact that gate receipts account for 1/4th or more of the total revenues with sponsorship being the higher contributor.

Figure 13- Dependence on Gate receipts (euro million) in Europe and UK

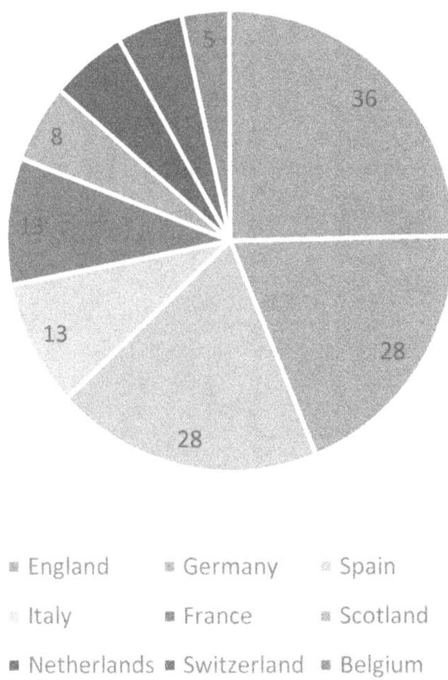

Source: UEFA Club licensing benchmarking report

Figure-13 provides the average gate receipts per club in 2017-18 in euro million.

The figures (in euro million) when read by country names in descending order are:

England-36; Germany-28; Spain-28; Italy-13; France-13; Scotland-8; Netherlands-8; Switzerland-7 and Belgium-5.

Countries like England, Germany, Spain have high gate collections.

Figure 14- Net profit (%) of profitable clubs in UK and Europe- 2017-18

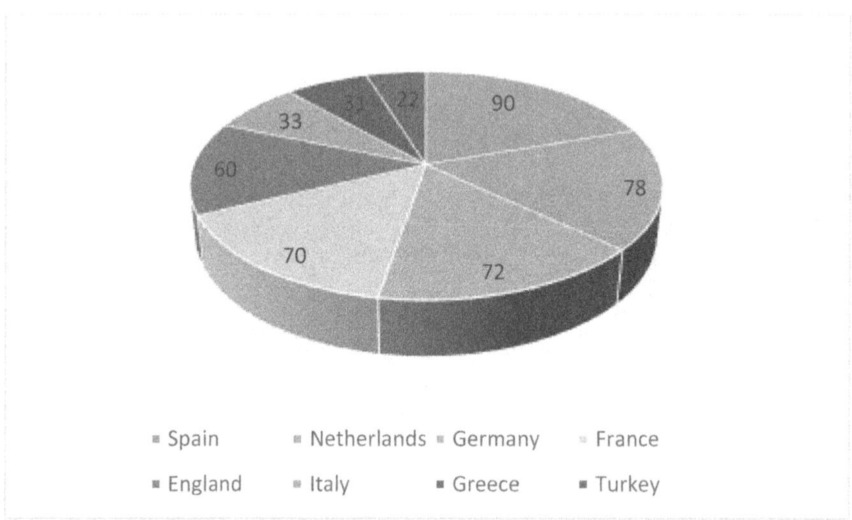

Source: UEFA Club licensing benchmarking report

Figure-14 shows the share of profitable clubs to be varying widely across leagues. Amongst the country-wise clubs that recorded net profit in year 2017-18 (represented in % terms), Spain ranks high (90) followed by Netherlands (78), Germany (72), France (70), England (60), Italy (33), Greece (31), Turkey (22).

Cricket stadiums

Cricket stadiums in India are generally flocked by a minimum of 30000 and a maximum of 80000 spectators for high quality matches. This would get dwindled by $1/3^{rd}$.

Unverified sources point to as much as Rs.10000 crores as the loss in revenue by not playing the IPL (Indian Premier League) in India.

The impact in India will also be felt across other sporting leagues of Badminton, Football, Tennis, Golf, Kabaddi, Hockey, etc.

Traders

Shop keepers and other roadside vendors fall under this definition. Displaying and vending smaller items require more care. Buying a glass bottle or a saree material, unless touched and felt the sale would become improbable. Shops in India or on the roads are crowded irrespective of whether a sale is announced or not.

- How would one effect payment: digitally?
- Does this mean that roadside vending may get disallowed?
- What would the fate of these traders be?
- Would they shift onto a different profession?

Venture capitalists

Investors in venture capital funds would have to embrace an extension from an 8-10 years' investment by an additional 3-4 years to tide over the current crisis and stay supportive of the management with exits getting stretched. In the past 3 years the transactions have been worth about 3.3 billion USD.

CHAPTER-5

ENTREPRENEURSHIP, TRADE, TRADE BARRIERS

Consultants

Consultants have a golden opportunity as deal makers. For many firms to come out unscathed is going to be a far cry. Many companies may decide to hive off divisions, factories in part or full or even get their company merged or acquired to overcome the crisis. In many cases of start-ups, it is down rounds now that of mobilization of the much needed capital at lower valuations. On either side of whether a buy or sell, a consultant stands to gain. It is bumper time for them over the next 12-18 months.

Consumerism

Chat bots to find direct channel to consumers

How we change our consumer behavior and business models are likely to persist after the Covid-19 crisis abates.

When it comes to food, grocery and other goods from brands, chat bots may start selling products directly to consumers on What's app. This will possibly reduce dependence on e-commerce platforms.

How will this be different?

Consumers will choose products, quantities and delivery slots in a what's App chat with an AI (Artificial Intelligence) Bot instead of an e commerce platform. This will reduce footfalls in retail outlets further keeping up the social distancing norms.

This is different from the usual dependence on aggregators with change from B2B (Business to Business) to D2C (Direct to Consumers). Consumers will be happy to receive their supplies directly from the brands they trust instead of having retailers in between.

The chat bot can do everything from payments and tracking shipping to showing recommendations of all the conveniences with promptings. The difference in most chat bots are that they are non-transactional. These chat bots are conversational AI (Artificial Intelligence) interfaces which is transactional.

In future, it may be hard to run call centers because it shall require people to go into offices, manage from their dedicated spaces, telephones and computer equipment's that can track and analyze calls. Post Covid-19, these centers can run by automating them. The demand for business continuity has spiked in this environment leading to a variety of changes.

Resistance to do business with a rising China

India and its start-ups have long gained with Chinese funds. More than 2 dozen Chinese firms have funded 92 Indian start-ups. China has been India's fastest growing FDI in the past 5 years. It has poured money into e-commerce, technology, retail, automotive and manufacturing sectors.

In 2012, Chinese investment in India was just $102 million. The current estimates of Chinese FDI in India is between $5- $8 billion.

According to a Gateway House report in Feb'20, Chinese tech investors led by Baidu, Alibaba, Ten cent (BAT) have invested $4 billion into Indian start-ups and funded 18 of 30 Indian unicorns (start-ups with billion dollar valuations) in the last 5 years. Indian start-ups like Paytm, Byju's, Oyo, Ola, etc. have been beneficiaries.

Chinese investments rank 18th highest in India's FDI inflows from countries, up from 24th in 2014 and 35th in 2011.

The fear is accentuated by the fact that many of the Chinese investments have come through third countries like Mauritius, Singapore, Hong Kong. The Chinese investments in start-ups have raised data security and privacy concerns too.

Smartphone market in India is dominated by Xiaomi and Oppo who hold the fast-growing market of nearly half billion size.

Should in case China exercise extra caution hereafter and is subject to clearances by the Government of India, this would get the lossmaking Indian start-ups to immediately start seeking alternative sources of funds or face collapse.

Recently India has blocked the automatic route for investments from nations that share a land border to prevent "opportunistic takeover/ acquisitions" of vulnerable Indian companies as stock markets plunged during the coronavirus pandemic."

Few other countries –Australia France, Germany also want to protect the undervalued companies from Chinese grasp.

Consumer behavior for goods and services in India

Demand for roti (food) is on but not for kapda (clothing) and makaan (housing). Since most households in India are engaged in informal jobs, with a substantially large segment either poor or vulnerable to poverty for lack of savings, there are limits to how much household expenditure can be managed.

Everyone will demand health goods – from face masks, test kits, hospital beds, ventilators, etc.

Many will stop buying non-essential durable goods –from small ticket items like clothes, shoes and beauty products to big ticket items like white goods, cars, apartments, etc.

Demand may not change much towards foodstuff, hygiene products, medicines, cell phone talk times, etc.

Consumer behavior – post Covid-19[11]

The fear of the disease will continue to linger for long. One may shun shared cabs and public transport. It is possible that one may start using private transport and there can be surge in demand for mass market cars.

Consumers may shift to big branded hotels as the popular perception is that homestays may lack in hygiene and sanitation standards. In many cities, the Indian Government had directed many of the hotels to provide rooms for returning immigrants and also to quarantine patients who are undergoing treatment. This can be a stigma for the future guest. The shared spaces and rented properties may undergo negative changes in demand.

People may get wary of going to overcrowded shops and hence online grocery companies and ecommerce companies may pick up on their pace.

With major malls and restaurants, cinema theatres and retail shops down, major readjustments in operations and finances may be

---

[11] Bansal Shuchi, Article- Consumer behaviour, mint,02/04/20, pg. - 5

required never before imagined by them.

A Nielsen study unraveled the following consumer attitudes by looking at retail purchase in traditional, modern and e- commerce channels.

When the disease first got tracked in India and a lockdown was announced, there was a significant increase in consumer interest in health and hygiene products, leading to purchase of safety items such as hand sanitizers and face masks.

As the disease spread, consumers started stockpiling their pantry with staple food and assortment of health and safety products. More store visits and size of basket expanded.

Quarantine stage started with higher online shopping. The provisions and groceries were stacked up from 1-3 months, unsure of the fear of supplies.

Nielsen predicts that, post lockdown, people would be more cautious about health and there could be permanent shifts in supply chain and increased usage of e-commerce.

People may step out to carry out shopping and seek restaurants, but not at the same pace and regularity of visits as before.

The poor buying sentiment of consumers will have to be overcome by discounts, cashbacks, bank and digital wallet offers. Big large apparel retailers, other big brands and ecommerce majors may roll out huge discounts across categories as soon as most markets and malls reopen. With improvement in supply chains, operation costs will go down and these savings may be passed on to consumers as benefit.

The costs of operating a ride hailing company with the changed sanitation standards will become higher but consumers would have no choice but to seek and absorb them.

Hygiene protocols and how brands are executing them through each and every touch point will dictate how consumers start basing their purchasing decisions and fix a price.

Demand for household appliances

Post the Covid-19 crisis, the question as to whether housemaids are required is a question mark.

The room cleaning robots, washing machines and dishwashers will gain more acceptance. This calls for a one-time capital expenditure. The other day I came across a vegetable cleaner, which is sort of washer cum cleaner when placed in a sort of vending machine, though much smaller in size and is aimed at improving hygiene standards.

While it is universally known that demand for goods and services shall be reduced in the times to come, the change in demand composition is yet to be deciphered.

Fitness centers

The massive investments made by fitness centers across the country might see a lull. With social distancing and fitness equipment requiring cleaning, how these would get managed is anybody's nightmare. It cannot be crowded anymore.

Sequencing of members / participants in a queue is a pre –requisite. Daily visits may be a thing of the past. Revenues of these centers will also fall. It is possible that the more affordable set of individuals and their families may decide to buy their own set of equipment each suiting their family member based on their age and sex. It is possible that the many open-air gymnasiums provided by the State Government in parks may be in higher demand fearing the risk of contracting infections in clubs and stand-alone gymnasiums.

FMCG (Fast Moving Consumer Goods) industry

The long-term effects of the pandemic will have widespread impact in the months to come lasting for a year or so.

AC Nielsen counts 52 cities as metros or those with a population of more than a million. Shoppers in India's metro cities will increasingly be shifting to supermarket chains, and even ordering their groceries online, prompting the two organized retail formats to corner a bigger share in the sale of fast moving consumer goods in a country where local grocery stores still control a bulk of the market. In all the two formats now account for roughly 30% of FMCG sales in the country's metros.

FMCG companies will also create delivery partners to fill gaps in distribution.

Driverless vans have started delivering groceries in lower traffic areas.

Geo political circles[12]

As per a published newspaper article, geopolitical trend lines were discernible but the current pandemic has only speed highlighted to define the broad contours of the emerging global disorder.

---

[12] Sood Rakesh, Article- Geopolitical circles, The Hindu, 11/05/2020, pg. -6

(a) Asia on a high, USA at a low

Post 2008 financial crisis, with the resilience that was visible, what became clear was the rise of Asia. Economic historians pointed to its inevitability as until 18th century, Asia accounted for half of the global GDP. The industrial revolution and naval expansion led to the West gaining stream then which is possibly getting reversed. Economic forecasts indicate that out of the G-20 countries, only China and India are likely to register growth in FY20-21, however small it might be.

Asian countries have also handled the disease better than the US and Europe. Consequently, Asian economies will recover faster than those in the West.

(b) USA takes a step back

The USA had played a decisive role for long time since World War I. This time it felt short and had to manage its resources which critically fell short of the citizen's expectation. President Trumps policy shift to 'America first' during his election rhetoric has suffered as they were left to corner supplies of scarce medical equipment and medicines and acquiring biotech companies engaged in R&D which has possibly pushed it to what is called as 'America alone'. On the contrary, the policies pursued to show aggression in Iraq and Afghanistan has become domestic political quagmires which President Obama had mentioned as "leading from behind".

(c) Dissent and non-commonality within EU (European nations)

The old Europe and new Europe have different ideologies which is hard to bridge. Lack of cohesion as visible during the Brexit negotiations, setting up a Covid-19 fund to be funded by the European Union, etc. clearly show discord. The Intra European rift is getting wider and its relations with Russia and China is always complicated. Strains show up when austerity measures were imposed on Greece, Italy, Spain and Portugal by the fiscally conservative Austria, Germany, Netherlands.

During this pandemic Italy did not get the support of few EU neighbors and finally China had to send medical teams, critical supplies of medical kits. Schengen visa or free border movement has become a victim to the pandemic.

(d) China gains further

At the turn of the century, China joined the WTO (World Trade Organization). China under the current regime is becoming more assertive and is assuming more global responsibilities. In recent years, the US-China relationship moved from cooperation to competition to confrontation. The partial economic de-coupling will gather economic momentum as the US election season nears. Xi-Jinping, the Premier might continue beyond 2022   and his signature Belt and Road initiative seeks to connect China to the Eurasia and Africa through both maritime and land routes by investing   trillions of dollars in infrastructure building as a pre-emptive move against any US's attempt containment. The confrontational rivalry with US may intensify.

(e)   Organizational reputations at risk

The World Health Organization (WHO) has fallen prey to the global pandemic for not having understood the impact and multi-dimensional factors that was visible at the early stage of the virus in Wuhan, China.

The UN Security Council (UNSC), G-7, G-20 is ineffective too and have always been subject to power politics. There is a long felt need for reform of these bodies through collective global leadership.

(f) Fallout of nations from volatile energy market

Energy markets were getting fundamentally altered with the US emerging as major energy producer along with its consent to hasten up green technologies and renewables on account of climate changes concern. With depressed oil prices, post the likely recessionary trend that is emerging, will fuel further tensions in West Asia countries which are dependent on oil revenues. Now, with the deepening of rivalries, the conflicts can create political instability where the local regime is fragile.

Gold as a safe haven in turbulent times

Higher risks and free flowing liquidity from global central banks make gold a favorable asset during concerning times.

Figure 15- Comparison equity Index vs Gold price movement in India over 20 years

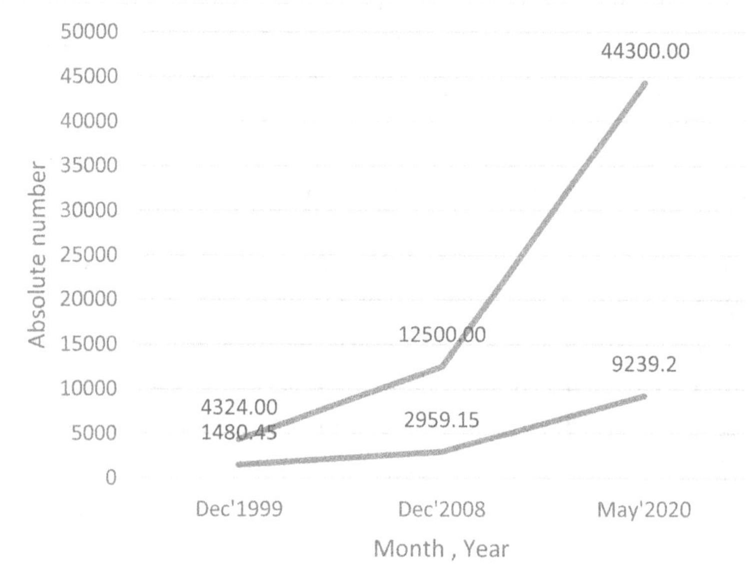

Figure -15 demonstrates comparison made between Nifty 50 stock index (bottom line- blue) and Gold prices (top line-brown) at differing points, which periods are chosen as crisis periods, i.e.; Dec 1999 is just prior to dotcom bust, Dec 2008 is prior to the economic crisis and May'2020 is the period when the pandemic is on.

During this period, gold prices, per 10 grams, have shot up by almost 10 times (4324 to 44300) while equity stock index has moved up (1480.45 to 9239.2) by about 6 times. The co-relationship between economic crisis, financial risk and Gold gets established.

Growing with steady demand

Demand happens as the way demand is projected only by looking at the supply side. In a published newspaper article[13] it has been summarized how Indian households earn, save, live, think and how they access public goods as follows:

1. India's household consumer demand is vulnerable and skittish because of dismal occupation demographics, lowly paid and uncertain livelihoods for most and because most Indian households have very little "surplus income ", money remaining after covering their routine expenditure, leave alone their non-routine requirements and emergencies. Most consumer demand experts have been reluctant to link poor occupational demographics to lower consumer demand beyond monsoon and the double whammy impact of demonetization and GST on small traders and businessmen.

2. In terms of demographics, the following is to be understood:

Migrant-daily wage workers - 32% of Indian households and who contribute to 24% of India's household expenditure; Middle class-20% of households account for 36% of consumption expenditure.

The table below maps the consumption expenditure based on share of household consumption expenditure contributed by different occupational groups further divided into the income level they live in. Income bands of rural households is classified as: Poorest, Middle, Richest.

India's household consumption behavior

Rural households account for 57% of all India household

---

[13] Bjiapurkar Rama and Shukla Rakesh, Article- Growing wallet not giving up, Mint,20/04/2020, pg. -1,12

consumption expenditure while urban household consumption accounts for 43% of total consumption. Rural households account for 54% of household income while the rest is contributed by the urban households. The data given below has been published in a financial newspaper.

Table 7- % share of total household expenditure with respect to rural consumption

Sl no	Main occupation / source of household income	Poorest- 40% = no surplus income	Middle -40% = aspirational Indians, spend more during good times and curtailing during bad times	Richest- 20% = better earners and spenders	Overall - rural
1	Farming and allied agriculture business	7.5	13.6	9.2	30
2	Non-farm micro business owners , individual service providers, petty cash traders, small shop owners	2.5	5.0	6.1	14
3	Salaried job, self-employed professionals	1.6	5.9	10.6	18
4	Casual labour of all kinds	15.3	13.8	0	29
5	Other sources (remittances, pensions)	20	3.0	3.9	9
6	Total	29	41	31	100

Source: ICE 360 degree India household surveys (2014,2016); 2018 samples. Note: Figs in Red – totally at risk; Black – partially at risk; Green – relatively safe

ACBC – (After Corona Before Corona)

Explanation:

Good harvest and a good market helps 30% of rural expenditure as per sl no 1.

- Sl no 4,5 gives us an understanding that casual labour (29+9 -3.9) or about 34% will come under stress when remittances from migrant labour is affected
- Sl no 3- with 18% shows that the salaried in rural India are in formal employments which are in safe category.
- Overall, Sl no 1,2,3 equals 62% of rural spends will happen if agricultural activity can get done.

Table 8-% share of total household expenditure with respect to urban consumption

Sl no	Main occupation / source of household income	Poorest- 40% = no surplus income	Middle -40% = aspirational Indians, spend more during good times and curtailing during bad times	Richest- 20% = better earners and spenders	Overall - rural
1	Salaried people and self-employed professionals	6.3	17.1	19.4	43
2	Petty trade/ shop vendor / individual service provider / shop owner / businessmen	7.2	12.7	9.1	29
3	Casual labour	8.2	9.5	0	18
4	Agricultural Income	1	15	1.2	4
5	Rent, investments, remittances from abroad, etc.	1	2	2.6	6
6	Total	24	43	33	100

Source: ICE 360 degree India household surveys (2014,2016); 2018 samples. Note: Figs in Red – totally at risk; Black – partially at risk; Green – relatively safe

Explanation:

- Job security will be low in urban households as they could be less formal than rural
- Sl no 1, 19.4% is dominated by high income groups, primarily salaried is safe. This class of people abstain from luxury and will maintain it for a while. They will spend only when persuaded by suppliers.
- Job losses and restructuring will be rampant in the rest of the consuming class.
- Sl no 2, half of the consumers about 15% will not be at risk as they are small businessmen, micro entrepreneurs and service providers. Even if they liquidity, they will be careful spenders as they might carry loan burdens.
- Sl no 4, 5 equals (4+6 -1) or 9% live on agricultural income, depend on remittances from abroad and pension income is safe on the consumptions.
- About 52% of urban consumption might hold itself as in safe category.

Overall summary of Tables 7 and 8

- 58% of household consumption will happen, contributed by rural at 61% and 39% by urban India.
- Lower food inflation coupled with urban salaried jobs if protected might help us to sail through
- Agricultural season is a crucial factor at play

ACBC – (After Corona Before Corona)

Business owners and employers

Many experienced business owners who were optimistic for the last 6 quarters despite talking in hushed tones about the slowdown were fairly sure that their industrial enterprises will thrive, albeit temporary shocks. How is it that within 4 weeks, all the business owners were seeking governmental support for survival is a mystery. Panic, gloom and despair seem to have taken center stage.

Most business owners did not see their businesses turning upside down though they did confide in the fact that their receivables are struck but did not see the world-upside down.

Now, post the outbreak and the lockdown, the new mantra (solution) is cost cutting. This seems to be a herd mentality at both extremes. Human mind is always myopic of the present and is biased for the present.

A management professor, Prof. Tulsi Jayakumar in a published newspaper article[14] says that cost cutting at this juncture is akin to going out food-shopping when you are particularly hungry. It would trigger binge-cutting of the worst variety, setting off a chain of pandemic-like economic consequences leading you down a spiral.

"Possibly, no panic and optimism are the new lower normal with miseries shared and not socialized among workers alone. This would help others thrive, so that you may survive not just today, but well into the future." is the view of the expert.

It is possible that business owners underestimated the virus and were more attuned to guiding us from one quarter to another.

---

[14] Jayakumar Tulsi, Article in mint

So, where lies the vision, the conservatism and forecasting of learned intellectuals and individuals seated in the corner room?

Make in India –push

With a large local demand, lower corporate taxes to set up new industries announced recently, the plan is to market Brand India when the country's FDI inflows have fallen 1.44% on y-o-y basis to $10.67 billion in FY'20.

The Government is creating a guide for potential investors on how quickly they can invest in the country with low capex models to operate in select clusters being identified across 9 cities which are considered attractive for investment.

Greater-Noida cluster could be an electronics hub and Hyderabad a hub for pharma and vaccine. Besides, Ahmedabad, Vadodara (Bharuch-Ankleshwar cluster), Mumbai –Aurangabad, Pune, Bengaluru, Hyderabad, Chennai, Tirupati-Nellore are the other most attractive clusters for investors.

These clusters have been identified based on sectoral requirements and tax incentives to promote the country as an alternative business continuity plan destination amid the ongoing Covid-19 pandemic.

According to recent reports, in the midst of long-term structural shift from China, several companies prefer to locate to other South East nations due to the unpredictability of governments and bureaucratic actions and policy revisions.

Market Research

The methodology is likely to change with face to face interviews giving way to online research as in the West.

Digital research also will grow rapidly. However, majority of research like mystery shopper services and product trials cannot be moved online.

The scope for online research will increase as every company will be looking at enhancing its brand and consumer reach as consumer behavior will change significantly soon.

Loan products, entertainment, retail and auto segment will resort to research in a big way, post the Covid-19 lockdown.

Online liquor sales

Reportedly 57 million people are dependent on alcohol consumption. The harmful effects of liquor are such that 40% and 72% are the road accidents in city and highways respectively due to drivers being under the influence of alcohol.

In 2016 India happened to be the world's top market for whisky at 193.1 million out of 393.2 million sold worldwide. The total market size in 2019 of liquor is USD 48 billion.

About 15-20% of states revenues, some Rs.2.48. lakh crores come from levies on alcoholic beverages. Possibly, online sales of liquor could be a necessity as there are many who are alcoholic dependent but cannot step out in view of continued restrictions during the pandemic. There is always a fear of proliferation of spurious liquor. People suffering from alcoholic withdrawal may have to get hospitalized. To overcome these constraints, it would become a better option to promote online and offline sales with higher excise duty.

Many an attempt made by start-ups to vend online sales of alcohol has not met with success due to Excise (tax) department who have cited laws that have not caught up with newer business models.

Possibly, online sales and home delivery option will reduce drunken driving.

Brick and mortar shops are wary of online shopping as they pay huge license fee to states. These concerns can be assuaged by allowing online delivery aggregator from the brick and mortar shops and imposing stricter territorial limits as in the case of medicines. States can possibly recoup lost license fee from corresponding increase in online sale license fees. The reluctance to sell online is also coming from selling to under aged as per a published newspaper report on online liquor sales.[15]

Restaurants

There are 7.3 million employed and is an industry which is the second largest employer of human capital in India after agriculture but one which will be the last sectors to open up. There would be timing curbs on dining.

Retailers

Retailing as a business is not categorized as a MSME but has 13000 organized retailing operating with more than 5. lakh outlets have 900 billion USD revenue in India does not come under the MSME fold. Retailers will hesitate to take higher inventory. Larger companies may take 6 months to revive and 12 months for the smaller retailers. Retailers are possibly sitting with 6 months of unsold inventory. Apparel manufacturing industry has 12 million employees, with 7 million in the domestic sector while retail has 46 million employees out of which 6 million are in modern retail.

---

[15] Taneja Aman and Rastogi Anirudh, Article- Online liquor sales, Economic Times, 25/04/20

Salaried employees

In future, companies will up the ante further and increase the variable salary component and link them to their company's performance.

Where the question arises between layoffs and salary cuts, the latter is better as per economics Prof Moorthy, IIM-B. The entire pain borne by the country in this looming crisis can be brought down by sharing it across the society. He has suggested that the Central Government reduce its employees' salaries by 30% and advocates the private sector to do the same. This should be further subjected to a proportionate cut possibly by reducing rentals and school and college fees. By carrying out such a move, the overall cost levels which are high in our country all across the spectrum can be reduced. Only the pensioners need needs a look into and that can be overcome by providing a higher interest rate on their safe deposits. In effect this will help target inflation as price rises will be kept under check.

With increased performance orientation and decision making as the routine, the proportion of fixed costs is likely to see a drop. Companies will start conserving cash for immediate business requirements. The variability factor may kick in to link the variable pay out to company performance over a longer duration than just the immediate results.

This would become more applicable to sectors like fintech, FMCG, IT, pharma, e commerce, etc. Where performance is dropping due to external factors too, the fixed cost burden will reduce thus allowing the company from laying off, reducing salaries while protecting job losses.

Since the costs are higher at the middle and senior level, greater individual accountability for leading the organization through tougher times becomes a necessity which should be viewed with an elastic payment.

Employees at entry or lower level may have just about 5-10% as variable while it could be 10-20% at junior management / experienced individual contributors, 20-30% for middle management and 30-50% for top management across industry sectors as per Willis Towers Watson, well known HR (Human Resources) firm.

Social security for gig workers

The Government is contemplating issuance of an ordinance to ensure a social security scheme for gig workers, platform workers and other unorganized workers foreseeing significant increase in the numbers post Covid-19 outbreak which has raised unemployment. This move will benefit delivery boys of e- commerce companies, cab drivers, day to day helpers, rickshaw pullers, roadside vendors etc. Possibly, the Government, the worker and the employer will jointly contribute to this scheme which has 500 million work force and is growing by about 17% year on year.

Solar and Wind Energy

India now has 33GW (Giga Watts) of Solar and 38GW of wind power. India seeks to produce 100 GW from solar projects and 60GW from wind power plants by March 2022. The lockdown cut pollution levels in India and influenced local weather helping improve solar radiation and wind patterns and bringing better output to solar and wind energy developers.

Testing Covid-19 rationally[16]

In India, a hot spot is defined as a location with 100 Covid-19 positives. Most believe that the real number could be far higher. Mass testing would require a huge outlay and may not be the obvious choice.

There is low probability just by doing random testing which may not help in picking the infected person. It is found that there will be a large number of false positives while negative test results will be accurate.

The experts in a published newspaper article are of the view that there should be clinical symptoms before undertaking testing as mathematical probability proves that the test kit should be over 90% sensitive, and one has to do it twice.

Tourism

The absence of immediate funds can lead to job losses, bankruptcies and destruction of the tourism model as per Confederation of Indian Industry. The economy could lose revenues of about Rs. 5 trillion in the next year and with 38 million jobs at stake.

Trade deficit - India

Exports have shrunk in 28 of the 30 sectors due to large scale supply chain disruptions. Table-9 provides the shrinking exports and imports in India.

---

[16] Datta Santanu and Ghosh Mrinal.K, Article- How to test Covid-19 rationally, Economic,Times,16/05/2020

Table 9- Exports, Imports, Trade Deficits in India- April'2020

April 2020	Value ($ billion)	Growth (% year on year)
Exports	10.36	-60.28
Imports	17.12	-58.65
Trade deficit	6.76	

Source: GOI data

The Trade deficit has shrunk from 15.33 USD billion to 6.33 USD billion. The World Trade Organization (WTO) has projected that global merchandise trade will plummet between 13% and 32% in 2020 due to the Covid-19 outbreak.

Central bank and its role in printing money

As per a recent published newspaper report[17], "this is the time for wartime financing, and normal rules cannot apply. Printing money will generate demand, kick start projects, help businesses and employees and workers. And given the steep economic dip, risks of overheating are trivial. Government of India and RBI must opt for printing money. Procedural caution may kill the India story."

Herein below, we analyze what major economies around the world are doing and the benefits and risks of printing currency.

---

[17] Economic Times, Article, 01/05/2020, pg. -9

Printing of money has the following options:

Option 1: Central Bank buys government debt / bonds: This is done to inject cash into economy. This is akin to printing new money though done electronically.

Option 2: Central Bank purchases private sector bonds: Seller is able to get rid of illiquid assets. Cash generated can be redeployed.

What are major economies doing?

Central Banks	Measures
US federal reserve	Printed money to counter 2008 crisis and using the same template now
European Central Bank	Printed money, removed the limit on bonds it can buy from any single Eurozone country
Bank of England	Ready to temporarily lend money to Government, if needed
Bank of Japan	Has pledged to buy unlimited amount of government bonds

In India, the risks of printing money bring with it high inflation and high current account deficit, depreciation of currency and a higher Non Performing Assets (NPA's) as a consequence. The current day benefits of printing currency are possibly high due to lower demand for goods and services, cautiousness of borrowers, low trade and lesser concern on current account, lower crude prices and economists worry of deflation which is structurally more worrisome than inflation.

In 2008, post the financial crisis what India did was slightly different as given under:

- Debt monetisation by RBI was the norm in 1980s and until late 1990s;
- Government deficits were monetised through ad hoc treasury bills
- In 1994, curbs were imposed under an RBI-government pact
- Were completely phased out after 1997
- But it continued in another form-with RBI picking up unsubscribed public, debt action
- FRBM Act'2003, barred RBI from buying primary issuances of government debt.

It is a tightrope walk for Indian policy makers as interest rates can rise sharply if demand picks up and the concerns of a sovereign downgrade. Both lack of credit or higher interest rates can kill an industry. The financial markets cannot support higher borrowings in excess of the budgeted expenditures.

Transformative changes

Businesses may have opened, but gymnasiums, swimming pools, cinema halls, schools and colleges may be shut for long. Over 300 million Chinese students in schools and colleges, universities are taking classes online every day and all kinds of new learning platforms, teaching everything from classical music to Pilates, are now booming.

Travel and tourism will be the hardest hit and will be a having longer tail to recover. In China, a nucleic acid test certificate is required to check-in into a hotel. If one is a foreigner, he may be denied booking. In the absence of the test certificate, a hotel room is impossible.

Inter-city, Domestic travel will become expensive. Travelling to another city for work will most necessarily bring a 7-14 days' mandatory quarantine when one returns home. Travel for pleasure may become a thing of the past.

In China, most airline passengers are now decked out in not just masks, but full hazmat suits and goggles. Some airlines, like Emirates, carries out a pre-flight blood testing, with results issued in 10 minutes before one proceeds to obtain a boarding pass.

As a result of the continued closures and restrictions, many businesses are floundering. To get consumers to support them, some cities in China are now issuing 30 days spending vouchers to encourage people to support small businesses and retail. They are also making two –and –a half-day weekends the norm – perhaps one small silver of a silver lining to hold onto amid all the dark clouds.

Kindergartens

Pre-schools are those nursing pre kindergartens and lower kindergartens. They are used to train young children to get into the habit of going out of their homes and get attuned to a new environment.

Young toddlers have also not been spared by their school. Many children have been unwilling or are less able to adapt to online education. It is certainly a move that may not have resulted in effective teaching or learning scenarios. Teachers providing feedback to parents without physical interaction with children is unusual. We are seeing an unusual moment, "School-From-Home".

All of us are used to sitting together as toddlers and sharing our toys and books, in that order. Now, would it not be difficult to make these young children understand that they have to maintain hygiene and safer distances too. Unless you fall over each other, push and jostle each other where lies the fun at school.

In a published newspaper article[18] it is suggested that children at tender age during lockdown should be made to pursue self-directed learning like learning to cook, stroll around and observe in garden, play board games or an instrument to nurture multiple intelligences and make discoveries to have a lasting effect on their self- worth.

Internet- arming WFH with the best internet speed

Speed in internet is measured by Mbps (Megabits per second). The higher the Mbps the better off you are. The speed you want depends on what you use the internet for and how many devices will be using the service at once.

The average speed varies between 12 to 40 Mbps. Internet providers have different speeds between uploads and downloads. To figure out what sort of internet speeds you will need, break down your usage pattern:

- **Light use** – you use the internet for e-mails, basic video, reading news, voice calls and basic streaming.
- **Moderate use** – All of the light use categories are followed + one of the following: streaming HD video, multi-party video conferencing or online gaming.
- **High use**- All of the light use + some of the Moderate use.

---

[18] Rao Badami Divya, Article, P for Pandemic, The Hindu, 25/05/20, pg.- 11

If one is a moderate user, one is going to want to go with an average speed in the 12-25 Mbps speed. If one has 4 or more users or devices at a time, or one is frequently streaming 4k video or transfer large files, one should upgrade to high speed internet.

In India, number of daily active users in Microsoft teams have shot up from 44 million in March'2020 to 75 million in April'2020. India could quickly adapt to Zoom for both good (birthday, marriage) and for not so good events (interacting with patients, death ceremonies, etc.). Cloud collaboration tools are Zoom, Slack, Google hangouts, Google docs, etc. which are becoming increasingly relevant.

CHAPTER-6

GOVERNMENT, TECHNOLOGY

Aarogya Setu[19] - the universal gateway for a future ready India

India has introduced an App called the Aarogya Setu App which gets enabled with a smartphone with Bluetooth, with the location data on. It has a simple function to download personal details like mobile no, gender, age, address, date of birth, users travel history, contact history with a Covid-19 person. The Government has set an ambitious target of 350 million downloads which has over 61.3 million downloads (as on 20/05/20).

The App checks for symptoms and does the following:

- Indicates the zone where one is in, classified as green, orange, red.
- If the user is found to be at high risk due to any info provided by them, health authorities are alerted.
- App keeps a record of the devices it comes in contact with and in case those people test positive the user is alerted.
- A person tested positive does not have to key in details. Testing lab automatically uploads that data to the server, post which all recent contacts of the person are notified.

The App is likely to get adopted vide the following:

- Promotion through official channels like MyGov
- Companies and banks have been asked to push it to users

---

[19] Arogya Setu, Article, Economic Times, 20/04/2020

- Many firms are encouraging their staff to download the app
- Government is planning a massive celebrity led campaign on platforms like TikTok.

The challenges to the App are the following:

- Recent contacts of a Covid-19 positive person will only be traced and alerted if all of them have the app installed
- App not integrated with all mobile operating systems
- App does not tell users if they are in a hotspot zone or how many people around them are positive and at what distance
- Functionalities like updating hotspot data and matching it with location are being added.
- Too many personal data are to be uploaded to activate the app. The security of the data uploaded has been questioned in view of its privacy.

Now, let us understand the impact of Covid-19, on our lives, profession, sectors and on most aspects governing us:

Economy of India

The Indian economy is large and has a diversified sectoral base. The demographics and productivity are widely spread and are large and with stable domestic financing base. However, high governmental debt and wide fiscal deficit with weak physical, financial and social infrastructure could be dampener.

Credit Rating Agency, Moody's Investors Services expects Indian economy to grow at 6.6% in FY 22 after a gradual pickup in economic activity and demand later. The growth of the economy could be 0% in FY 21. The negative outlook has arisen due to growth risks, rise in non-performing loans from Banks and NBFC's. The fiscal deficit might hit of 10% of GDP in FY 21.

CRISIL, a ratings agency, believes it will be tough for India to return to its pre-pandemic growth levels at least for the next three years, irrespective of policy support. It estimates that under the base case scenario, India will suffer at least a 10 percent permanent loss to real GDP, assuming an average growth rate of 7 percent between fiscals 2022 and 2024. To be able to catch up to the pre-pandemic growth rates, India needs its average GDP growth to surge to 11 percent over the next three fiscals, "something that has never happened before," as per a note from CRISIL.

Even before Covid-19, India was staring at a serious economic slowdown with the GDP forecast lowered from 5% to 4.1% by several agencies. Recent reports suggest that the growth estimate will be further reduced to vary between 1.1% to marginally negative. India's unemployment rate as at end of May16th'2020 was staggering at a high of 24%.

Governments

In India, the Central Government coordinated the strategy and left the implementation part to the State Government during this pandemic crisis. Some of the State governments were not in office for too long and were in the midst of passing their annual Budgets when they were sprung with the management of the pandemic.

It is to be understood that many states met with success in managing the pandemic despite financial limitations that were exacerbated by significant unpaid tax dues from the Central Govt.

The Kerala State and its containment model has come for an appreciation thanks to its local level decentralization which has been a model for financial devolution and has focused its attention on the health of the education system and its well-meaning panchayat system.

The message here is to strengthen local level governance with operational, financial and planning autonomy.

It is time for the public health system to be strengthened at the local and tertiary levels. A big learning from this crisis is the absence of social protection for the poor and informal workers in particular. This is despite the fact that an overwhelming majority of workers are employed in the informal sector. Even where the social security is provided by law for construction workers, it barely exists on the ground. Hence, the Government must now fix this problem and enable social security for all such workers including migrant workers.

Similarly, the flaws in the food security architecture with overflowing granaries and hungry stomachs need to be looked into.

Possibly, the Government can take a leaf out of its success in many areas in this unprepared moment and emulate itself with success stories on the shortcomings of the recent past as mentioned in the earlier paragraph.

Governments world over have risen to the occasion and they run the show. The poor continue to live at the bottom of the pyramid, with or without Aadhar (a Govt. approved proof of identity document). Covid-19 is a public health crisis having immense political and economic ramifications. The previous endemic Ebola outbreak in 2014 played a major role in the US mid-term elections. A new study shows that the timing and the perceived threat of Ebola were significant factors in the Democratic party losing the elections in 2014. Is history repeating itself in the USA in 2020? Only time will tell.

In 2014, the republicans benefited from the situation because they exploited the Ebola fear in their campaign although US reported very few cases. They took their political advertisements to the hilt in their anti-immigration, anti-terrorism and anti-Obama rhetoric amplified the perceived threat. This was crucial in influencing voter choices as per a social media report. [20]

Bureaucrats

Bureaucrats are always known to maintain themselves well. Under the emerging circumstances, they may distance themselves more. Our bureaucrats will become even more powerful and more rules will only make an average citizens life more complicated. Possibly, license Raj can return to make it a compelling choice for the citizens.

In a published newspaper article[21] it is mentioned "as the circular flow of the economy has frozen, the job of getting the wheels moving again has become a dilemma of what comes first. Does supply kick start the circular flow or is demand a necessary precondition for resumption?"

Cloud Industry

The growth of this industry has been about 25% CAGR in the last 3 years. Demand for cloud services both at enterprise and consumer levels largely driven by WFH and being dependent on collaborative tools for group video conferencing, virtual schooling, entertainment and gaming, etc.

Microsoft teams has 44 million daily users, generating over 900 million meetings and calling minutes. Zoom cloud meetings is most downloaded app on android and IOS stores.

---

[20] The Virus of Fear: The Political Impact of Ebola in the US, bit.ly/ 35hJOBv

[21] Muralidharan Sukumar, Article, Mint, 09/05/20, pg-4

Netflix, Amazon Prime and Hot star which are streaming content on a cloud have also gained major traction. However, data security can be a challenge here

Jaspreet Bindra, an author, in his newspaper article[22] says that for India the cornerstones of the new golden quadrilateral would have content, carriage, customer and commerce. Further, he says that in the past content was owned by TV and studios, carriage was owned by telecom firms, customer was touched by multiple players and online retailers had commerce. To state an example, Amazon owned commerce and customer and Time Warner owned carriage and content.

In India, Reliance Industries Limited (oil major) and its group company Reliance Jio (mobile telephony) enjoy top ranking. During the pandemic, a notable deal got stitched between Reliance and Facebook-What's App, which may transform into something similar to the Chinese super app – WeChat which app is owned by Ten Cent Holdings that has integrated "apps within app" and provides for payment, ecommerce, taxi aggregator services, and food ordering.

This is via around a million third-party apps that run on its platform.

On the other hand, the Jio platform would include apps like Jio TV, Jio Saavn (music streaming), Jio News, Jio Cinema (video streaming), Jio Cloud, Jio TV+, Jio Health Hub, JioMoney (payment app), RJio (ecommerce).

---

[22] Bindra Jaspreet, Article, Mint, 01/05/2020

Benefits for Reliance Jio on the 4 cornerstones named above in the post Covid-19 era are the following:

Content- Jio and network 1 has vast libraries of movies, films and with the user generated content on face book and the platform it owns such as Instagram and What's App could be unparalleled.

Carriage – Jio has over 350 million wireless customers and is better placed than Airtel, its nearest rival. It may own every pocket of connectivity that the Indians so richly deserve.

Commerce- Amazon and Flipkart as e commerce companies own about 2% of the total retail market. Few large retail format stores may own another 3%.

In India, more than 90% of the retail trade happens through kirana (mom and pop) stores. With each of the shopkeeper using What's App and Facebook along with the Jio telecom network, Jio mart and a payment play would forge a strong relationship connecting millions of neighborhood stores to a billion consumers.

In the words of Reliance Industries Chairman, Sri. Mukesh Ambani, the Jiomart and What's App will facilitate and empower 3 crores small Indian kirana (mom and pop) shops to digitally transact with every customer in their neighborhood. In all, this deal has a win-win benefit: (a.) for customers who can get faster delivery of goods, (b.) for the government to collect taxes and (c.) the kirana (mom and pop) shops who can boost their turnover and (d.) help create new employment opportunities.

Customer – the customer owns us and not the other way around. Jio has the billing relationship with the customer which grants it direct access and data and has high exit barriers. The buying habits will help Facebook generate extraneous advertising revenues.

The article cum report compares the above to getting data, entertainment, food, shopping in one single platform and the verdict is that it replaces the old economy consisting of oil and mobility with data and content in the new economy. Clive Humbly, a mathematician in 2006 had said that in the new economy **"Data is the new Oil."**

Commenting on the Reliance Jio deal few authors including Prof V. Sridhar (IIIT-B) in their recent article[23] say that the biggest threat seems to be on the telecom players like Airtel and Idea-Vodafone, which can further loose subscribers due to various bundled services provided by the Super App. Thus, it is likely that there will be further stress in the telecom sector, which could lead to ouster of existing players. If this happens, it would be a serious problem in the telecom sector as competition will get further dwindled.

As per the study, Google, Facebook and Amazon have been nudging for a bigger pie of the digital advertising space. Since kirana (mom and pop) stores have not been advertising online, the face book Jio deal could be the game changer. Google has SME specific offerings – GMB (Google My Business), Digital Unlocked and Market Finder, to connect over a million businesses digitally.

With Chinese market out of bounds for these companies, India happens to be the next biggest market outside the US and by reaching out to the SME's especially for advertisements it would help them to understand the spending profile of millions of internet users/ consumers which in turn will get sold to businesses seeking to advertise for the right audience.

In the near future, all kirana (mom and pop) stores will be part of

---

[23] Sridhar V , Mehta Udai, Kumar Ujjwal, https://yourstory.com/2020/04/facebook-reliance-jio-deal-implications,29/04/2020

digital platforms. This will be the largest retail and consumer internet opportunities estimated to be more than $ 60 billion by 2025.

One would remember Covid-19 for a good reason: Reliance, as an innovator and a deal maker brought cheer to an otherwise sad phase of our lives to various constituents of the society by deploying M-POS (Merchant-Point of Sale) machines to create a hybrid online – offline e-commerce platform to be India's largest Omni-channel retailer.

Emerging nations and its impact on America:

India can become a more stable regional player if it can further improve its neighborhood ties.

In a column[24] in a newspaper - literary review, Stanly Johny says the US's relative decline is a secular trend as pointed out by Mr. Sreeram Chaulia in his book: Trumped : emerging powers in a Post American world.

According to him, the decline was visible even during the stints of Trump's predecessors. The difference with Trump is that he does not share the American establishments liberal internationalist worldview.

Since World War, American Presidents have played a key role in shaping the liberal international global order, which during the Cold war acted as a bulwark against the Communist bloc and thereafter as a US centric unipolar system.

---

[24] Johny Stanly, Literary Review, Hindu, 12/04/20, pg. -5

President Trump sees the liberal international global order as a "conspiracy concocted by liberal American elites to impoverish and suppress ordinary American people."

So according to Stanly Johny, Trump has adopted a neo-mercantilist, transactional capitalist policy that is rooted in American nationalism. This is Trump's America First doctrine, which practically precipitates America's decline as a global power.

"Russia and China have already established themselves as big powers in their immediate regions. Does the American decline mean that the world will again slip into a bipolar contest? or a tri-polar one."

There are emerging countries which could seize the moment.

"The path to a multipolar world never seemed less imminent than when Trump arrived on the scene", Chaulia writes in his book.

In the book, Chaulia identifies, four (4) such emerging powers – India, Turkey, Brazil and Nigeria. Therefore, while Chaulia's assessment about the decline of the US and the Trump opportunity holds true for our times, it is to be seen whether emerging powers, including India, is ready for the moment.

Digital innovations

Starbucks, for example was one of the first to introduce one of the best Omni-channel retail experiences through concepts like electronic payments, mobile apps, pick up only stores or third-party delivery networks to make ones' experience more ubiquitous.

The Starbucks mobile order payment app will allow customers to order beverages on their mobile and pick them up from the store, reducing the time spent in ordering them.

In India, they are trying to focus on delivery and launch India's first drive-thru-store to allow customers to engage with the brand in new and innovative ways.

Digital advertising, Social media

This industry is expected to cross Rs.50000 crores by 2025, while Indian digital ad spends stood at Rs.13683. crores in 2019 as per Dentsu Agencies Network. The majority of these spends go on social media platforms, followed by paid search, online video and display media. Facebook already leads the social media and bucket, while Google clearly has the search pie. With a stronger presence at the rural and grassroots level through JioMart, Facebook is likely to open up new opportunities.

Indian educational system in a digital world

How would schools and colleges operate physically? Difficult to imagine.

Covid-19 has forced the educational system to move online, in the USA, online courses provide an opportunity to hugely reduce the 1.5 trillion USD student loan problem. Almost half of student loans for attending private universities and 3/4ths of student loans for public universities go for paying rent and other living expenses.

Online university education will enable college students to stay at home with their parents, saving on rent, transport and other living costs. The sudden switch from classroom to online classes has affected quality. But if it continues for some more time, online classes will match with classroom teaching.

In India, high quality education can replace third rate education in third rate colleges. Virtual classrooms can be expanded without concerns of physical space for number of students. Large online classrooms can be further broken into smaller group of students with trained teachers who can facilitate online discussions. Access to international online education would give competition to even high quality Indian online education.

Movie releases vs OTT (Over-The-Top)

Many movie producers have been ruing their chances over their inability to release movies during the pandemic. Some of the producers have decided to opt for an alternate medium called OTT.

OTT media service is a streaming media service offered directly to viewers via the Internet which bypasses cable, broadcast, and satellite television platforms with proprietary equipment such as set top boxes.

Few of the movie theatres, movie distributors are fierce in their opinion and want to ban those releasing their movies on OTT. Manish Goswami, vice-president of Producers Guild of India, quoted in a newspaper: "Some producers are ready to wait. Some are willing to compromise with their profit and go for digital release. It is an individual choice. They should be allowed to do so. It is tough to calculate how much loss the producers have incurred, the amount would be massive as there are so many movies in pre-production, production and ready-to-be released stage."

Online learning

Recently the UGC (University Grants Commission) Chairman said that to maintain social distancing, online learning (e-education) is the only way out. This is a good measure and an exigent way to prepare for long closure of campuses.

Prof Shyam Menon in a published newspaper article[25] says there are

---

[25] Menon Shyam, Article, Online learning, The Hindu, 30/04/2020

many questions about the appropriateness of the long-term strategy for enhancing gross enrolment ratio in higher education:

1. How far will online education help support greater access to and succeed among the deprived class?
2. How equipped are digital forms of education to support the depth and diversity of learning in higher education?
3. Is there an unstated political motivation for this shift in strategy?

The offline education is one where students go through cultural barriers and overcome their anxieties by sharing and learning from their peer group.

Classrooms also has access to effective participation in language and social barriers. Some of these students who hail from rural parts also have to overcome their digital divide and constraints. Unless they receive consistent hand holding and backstopping, as per Prof Menon they would tend to remain on the margins and eventually drop out or fail. It is therefore necessary to think deeply and gather research based evidence on the extent to which online education can be deployed to help enhance the access and success rates.

What generally goes missing is to acquire practical skills, inquire, seek solutions to complex problems and learn to work in teams which involves direct human engagement- not just student-teacher interaction but peer-interactions.

Soon, a via media when found with digital forms of learning and engagement when clubbed with conventional form of education may give the necessary boost.

While around 85% of university students have access to the internet, only 41% are likely to have access at home. Among students from rural households, only 28% are likely to have access to have internet access at home. The gaps across states are significant. 51% of households in Kerala have internet access but only 23% have access at home. In AP, 2% have access to home while 30% are rural households which have access to internet.

In states like West Bengal and Bihar, only 7-8% of rural households have any access to the internet while access at home is miniscule.

Rural India – net users

The internet users in rural India currently at 264 million is likely to rise to an estimated 304 million in 2020, as per market research firm Kantar. The rise is spectacular as local language and video have been the key drivers

Impact on Education- a SWOT Analysis

Going from classroom to online for higher classes:

Many teachers, students, parents, left with no choice have quietly accepted online knowledge dissemination as the future and embraced it with both hands.

Possibly what was an alien concept and an elite way of learning is getting accepted as a concept.

The weakness in our system include lack of innovative thinking, inadequate infrastructure, untrained teachers, unequal accessibility, exam centric assessment and lack of learner autonomy.

The inequality and academic divide in India between the haves and have-nots could get divided further due to education going digital. Teachers in both private and government schools and their students in small cities and towns included should get prepared with access to computers and internet. Teachers in India are very adaptive and they might get used to Google classrooms and shall develop expertise to use them to conduct classes online.

The opportunities for online learning in India benefits :(1.) our students who belong to Gen Z (born between 1997 and 2010); (2.) numerous web resources; (3.) enthusiastic teachers.

Now, is the time to move our classes to a different platform, introduce e-learning and developing learner autonomy.

Teachers during the lockdown period have started sharing You tube links and videos and PPT's (Power Point) with their students and started engaging with them. This should be continued.

Many teachers starting from Montessori are using Zoom facilities and Blue jean meetings for online teachings and interacting with their students. These video conferencing facilities have features such as one -click scheduling, screen sharing and collaboration, cloud streaming and so on. Some educators have started to use Google Meet.

Google for Education Teachers Centers' online are distance learning facilities available. In countries where e-learning is popular, students have access to various online resources such as Massive Open Online Courses (MOOC's) which helps students, teachers and professionals upgrade their skills.

E-learning also helps in self learning without monitoring and intervention of teachers. Our country needs to take the threat of developed and developing countries seriously and lead the way in online education and promote it in right earnest. Administrators involved in education planning should give a serious thought to reducing the digital divide in the country and popularize digital learning.

Virtual is Virtuous

The post Covid-19 economy will render several jobs redundant. But it will also create many new jobs. It would create huge demand for online training courses on how to use online portals to provide the best services to clients, whether these are religious or medical or education related services.

Secure platform

Government of India may start working to create a secure platform as an alternative to Zoom for their own conferencing abilities. These might be in the form of Apps to be used all across government offices. This is important as Government has to make policies for hardware and software products to facilitate W-F-H. Use of personal devices to access official documents have raised cyber risks. Private users may also buy it from the developer once the efficacy of these Apps get proven with time.

There are two aspects to Working-From-Home:

1. How to use technology to allow seamless experience with an array of products including hardware and software that does not compromise on security standards;
2. Defining basic parameters of working from home.

Telecom sector - an essential service

India has a customer base of close to 1.2 billion (globally second to China) with 5.96 mobile towers and more than 22 lakh BTS (business telephone subscribers). Broadband connectivity is provided to 650 million subscribers

In the recent past, the telecom sector has been in the midst of controversies where everyone was looking down at the sector. At most times, the telecom sector has been seen as the cash cow and is the backbone behind all digital initiatives.

2020 is the landmark year for the telecom sector as it is the silver jubilee year of mobility services. After all digital is a combination of IT, electronics and telecommunications. About 6 % of the GDP comes from this sector.

This sector became the backbone of the country and ensured an uptime of 99.99% of their networks by maintaining key quality service requirements.

The local Governments and the State police department ensured diesel was supplied to DG sets acting as power back up at all towers and that uninterrupted power was provided to all data centers. Many sealed mobile towers were unsealed to make communications uninterrupted. Tele verification through IVR (Interactive Voice Response) was provided for new SIM's and mobile recharging outlets were allowed to be open. During the period of quarantine, the bottom-of-the-pyramid also received free voice and short messaging services.

During the pandemic, our economy and even the social sectors like health and education has leveraged the power of telecom to help all of us to be active. Even Governments have put up activities via digital mode.

If we are active socially, politically and economically, it is only through telecommunication in these difficult times. In our estimate, about 30-35% of the services sector which is live is only because of the telecom infrastructure. The lockdown has made all of us realize the power, importance and relevance of telecom in our lives.

Urban mobility

In the future, transport policymakers must keep cities moving through future disasters. A recent case study[26] provides insights on investments and strategies for operating public transport safely and developing pandemic resilient transportation management plans. The key lies in protecting the transport staff.

Public transport can even plug supply chain gaps and help small retailers, traders, migrant workers to move around. The case study authors suggested the following:

(a.) **Innovation of private sector to be leveraged –** Besides grocery deliveries, private mobility and technology companies can effectively contribute to pandemic management with government support by developing emergency systems for: facilitating peer-to-peer car- and ride-sharing, deploying self-driving cars, and even creating pop-up logistics matching retailers and warehouses with excess capacity.

(b.) **Prioritise for pedestrians and cyclists over cars-** During lockdown, bicycles and safe walking help combat accessibility crisis and physical inactivity. New York City, Mexico City, and Bogota can offer insights. As per the authors, reorienting land use to promote diverse transport modes and support micro-mobility is critical to reverse automobile demand, post pandemic.

(c.) **Food supply chains and urban logistics-** This pandemic has exposed food insecurity due to long supply chains which are prone to shocks. Diversifying supplier bases and sourcing locally could be a key. In the

---

[26] Chakraborti Sandip, and Hong Andy, joint study of Shenzhen, London, and France's, TGV, courtesy IIMA

words of the authors, Governments must incentivise firms who can overcome disruptions in business planning and promote urban or peri-urban agriculture by incentivising local production and consumption as key to pandemic-resilience.

Virtual courts

Courts may take up working in virtual manner to ensure justice delivery on matters pertaining to life and liberty of an individual which hearing cannot be denied at juncture as a pandemic. The parties desirous of taking up hearing through videoconferencing have to provide joint consent along with particulars of the matter. The virtual courts have to become user friendly and the lawyers and advocates have a huge gain to fill which we are sure they would.

CHAPTER-7
POPULATION, LIVELIHOODS

Households and industrial prospects - fight for survival vs flight to safety

A recent study comparing the periods Feb-April for year 2020 with year 2019 provides glaring comparison.

Figure-16 shows each financial instrument represented by two bars: on the left (blue bar -Feb-Apr'2019) vs on the right (brown bar-Feb-Apr'2020).

About Rs.8000. crores have been withdrawn by employees from government provident fund schemes since the lockdown which is unusual and is 10 times the amount of withdrawals. Investment related demand for gold has risen. Real estate transactions have come to a static halt.

In February-April'2020, currency with the public has risen by Rs.2.06. lakh crores which is a sharp rise over the Rs.1.08. lakh crores over a year ago for the same period.

The Figure below clearly indicates that many households have a dire need to shore up liquidity by digging into their retirement savings while many are moving towards safety of their savings and investments.

The rush to fixed deposits is attributed to fear of credit losses associated with other debt instruments. With people's inability to buy beyond essentials, monies are lying in short-term bank deposits.

Figure 16- Impact on household financial savings (net inflows/ outflows) during Covid-19 lockdown (Rupees. crores)

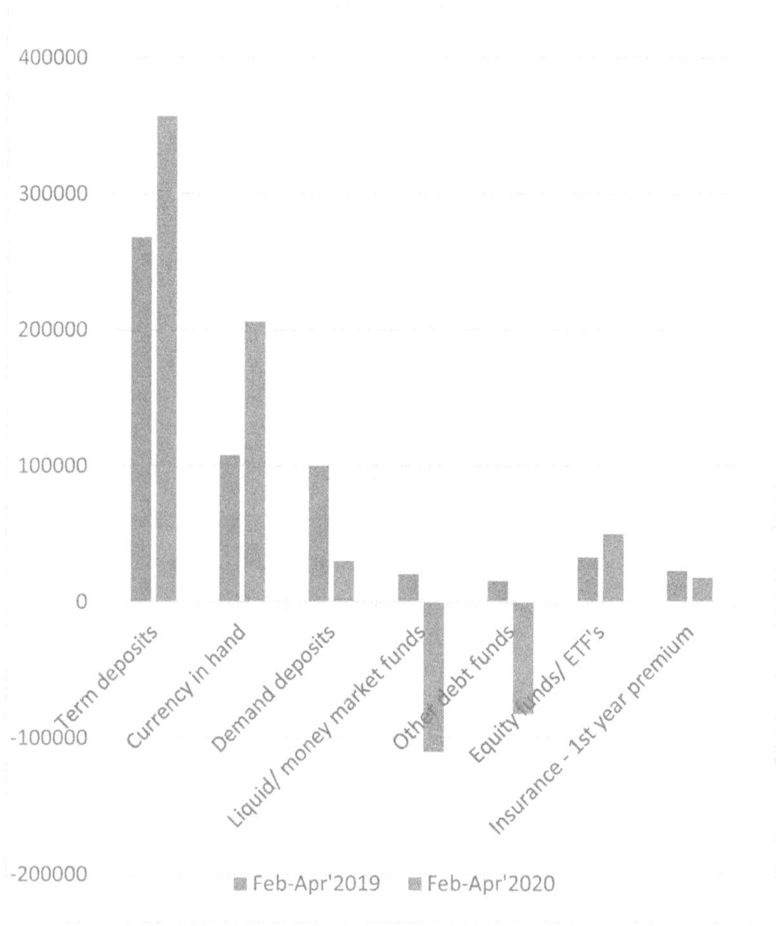

Source: RBI, AMFI, mint research

Crime

Experts opine that unemployment coupled with job losses and poor financial situation can lead to societal disharmony and create social unrest and increase in crime rate, post the pandemic.

Hair styling, saloon and spa

The lockdown helped men to grow longer hairs or avail of a haircut at home helped by their parents, spouse or children. Post lockdown the services may not be normal anymore as (i.) both the service providers and the beneficiary have to take safeguards and (ii.) to distinguish a salon and spa operator from that of a hospital care giver at all levels, may not be much different.

Lives vs livelihoods[27]

We may emerge from the pandemic with fewer lives lost but many individuals may be economically ruined as per an expert. And destitution, stress, suicide and crime could yet cause more deaths than the epidemic.

Jobs blood bath has already started in many industries and even the most generous employers have no choice but to reduce their workforce. Economists Renuka Sane and Anjali Sharma had studied cash holdings of 16300 non-financial firms with total annual sales of Rs.107 lakh crores (107 trillion) which is about 45% of India's likely GDP for 2020-21. Assuming revenues to be zero, wage costs at the same level (with no lay-offs), regular maintenance expenditure would be at 60% of normal levels, and with no change in interest payments.

Sane and Sharma found that 54.8% of these companies have 90 days or less before their cash runs out. In fact, 29.8% have 30 days or less to last with their cash. Without interest payments, the figures drop slightly to 47.5% and 23.4% respectively.

---

[27] Deb Sandipan, Article, Lives and livelihoods, Mint, 20/04/20, pg-11

In this set of vulnerable companies, whose sales total about 30% of GDP, 19% are large firms with assets worth over Rs.500.crs, and 53% belong to small-firm's categories with assets less than Rs.100.crs.

SME's employ 40% of India's workforce, but only large banks may get bank loans to tide over the crisis. It is not possible for a firm to immediately ramp up production and services to earlier levels, or get a large part of its customer base back.

There could be many large defaults coming up in the bank repayments from companies and firms. Post moratorium period, if loans get classified as a NPA, their lines of credit could be cut off permanently. This will aggravate the present crisis for both firms, companies and individuals who could possibly suffer from job losses, trade losses with meagre cash in hand.

India's consumption cum economic growth is accounted by the so called middle class which forms part of 35-40% of India's households. Most of the middle class and the upper middle class have low cash savings which possibly can last for 6 months without a regular income.

According to Motilal Oswal, a brokerage firm, between fiscal years 2013-14 and 2018-19, the real disposable income of households rose by 5.1% per year, while their real consumption expenditure rose by 7%. Household savings fell from 25% in 2013-14 to 20.7% in 2018-19 and 60% of those savings are locked in assets like real estate which suffers from illiquidity and is losing value dramatically. In 2018-19, household debt was a whopping 43.1% of real disposable income. Quite simply, the middle class does not have money, which led to the consumption slowdown over the past 2 years. With lockdown induced austerity and an uncertain future, Indians will consume less.

The pandemic will pass but economic devastation it will leave behind will last years and claim countless livelihoods/ lives.

Hospitality industry: Hotels, restaurants, pubs and bars

Job losses and salary cuts across sectors amid the pandemic will also severely impact the hospitality sector. People will not step into bars and pubs as they are typically overcrowded with social distancing becoming the new normal. Even discretionary spend will reduce. Restaurant industry has 7.3 million employees in India.

Contactless dining

Contactless dining is meant to eliminate the need for diners to touch valet receipts, menus and bill copies, when they are eating out. Safety, hygiene and trust will be the key aspects in winning customers. However, contactless dining needs to be commercially viable. If one is operating with all fixed costs at half the capacity, it is not sustainable.

The restaurant industry's turnover is about Rs.4. lakh crores. The number of people employed is about 7 million in the restaurant sector. Cloud kitchens may also feel the heat.

New health and safety challenges will be incorporated in hotels. Front desks in hotels will have protection shields in front desks, no buffets, mandatory mobile check outs and reduced banqueting capacity by 50%.

In China, for example, vide an April 12th directive from the National Health Commission, diners will have to be served meals in separate dishes. So, if three diners order a dish, it will be served to each separately to prevent the risk of infection. Bars and pubs would limit the number of patrons who can be present at any given time. Many restaurants may be unwilling to serve to foreigners because of the Governments call "rise in imported infections".

Medical stores

Pharmaceutical and medical stores have been advised not to sell paracetamol across the counter. It can be bought only with a medical prescription by submitting personal information of name, address, travel history so as to curb misuse and avoid self-medication.

Migrant population

Post the Covid-19, migrants may not be a welcome feature but will the elite give up the services of these invisible people, this fact remains to be seen in our daily lives.

Deployment of migrant labor and unorganized sector workers [28]

The government has an arduous responsibility of devising ways to support workers whose earnings have been destroyed during the last 2 months so as to maintain a supply-demand balance.

(a.)   Benefits provided and redeployment:
There are 450 million informal sector workers in India. More than 30 million work in garment industry, 11 million street vendors, 10 million construction workers, 7 million artisans, 6 million domestic workers.

Out of 450 million as estimated, it would be safe to assume that $1/4^{th}$ could be facing a daunting task to get back to employment or might have migrated.

---

[28] Sen Arijit, Article, Informal sector workers- displacement and reallocation of work, Economic Times

Government is trying to provide them food-for-work programme while they be recipients of cash transfers.

As a suggestion, the numbers who would still remain unemployed could be redeployed to (a.) look after quarantine centers and other treatment centers, (b.) join the textile industry to supply PPE's and masks. This could pave the way for these temporary class of workers.

(b.) Re-employment assistance based on requirement of demand:

For post pandemic producers of goods and services who enjoy uninterrupted demand there will be need to access stable input supply chains and marketing channels to rejuvenate their economic lives. The supply chains are mainly impacted in loading, unloading and transporting goods across borders. The unemployed class could be converted into dedicated transport workers (not drivers) who can transport raw materials, finished goods and people, if necessary, across districts and states and this is as essential as health workers. These people should be given adequate protective gear.

Local Immigrants

Based on a random estimate over 100 million people are circular immigrants in India. The job losses are difficult to predict. The major sub sectors using migrant labor are textiles, construction, stone quarries, mines, brick-kilns, small scale industry (diamond cutting, leather accessories, etc.), crop transplanting, sugarcane cutting, rickshaw pulling, fish and prawn processing, salt panning, domestic work, security services, sex work, small hotels, roadside restaurants, tea shops, street vending, etc. The economic contribution of migrants could be about 10% of GDP with internal remittances total long 7.485 billion USD in 2007-08. The remittances help the migrants to safeguard their families, ensure better quality of living and higher education of their children.

The states of UP and Bihar are the main sources while the states of Maharashtra, Gujarat, Delhi, UP, Haryana absorb these migrants. Southern Tamil Nadu has a lot of intrastate migrants. Coastal Andhra sees regular influx from Telangana and Odisha. Just 22 districts in the country account for. A third of all migrant workers.

The plight of the workers who lack social protection will remain the most crucial fallout of the pandemic India. It is unlikely that the migrants will forget the calamity and the difficulties experienced by them and they may take much longer time to return to places far away from their homes unless there are accessible insurance mechanisms in place for circular migrants in the informal economy. Some pregnant women migrants in India after waiting for days boarded public transport only to give birth enroute. Such has been their endurance and experience.

The Government will have to set up establishing proof of identity, citizenship, domicile status, place of work as well as registration for schemes so as to offer better safeguard to these migrants in the future. It is possible that there will be an increase in intra state migration in the future. We should only hope that the poor do not become poorer which then can have serious long-term impacts on economic growth.

Gulf immigrants

Over 12 million people are estimated to be migrants from south and south-east Asia. Of them, The Keralite migration pattern is a hugely popular and dominated number.

The twin shocks of a pandemic and an oil price collapse have jolted the Asia- Gulf migration corridor. Kerala as a state is expecting a decline in remittances by as much as 15% in the next few months. As per Shahjahan Madampat, a cultural critic and commentator based in

UAE states in a newspaper that," the exodus from the Gulf may be the first major manifestation of a reverse globalization and could cause lasting effects."

One-third of Kerala's income is accounted for by remittances from abroad which was more than Rs.1. trillion in 2019. It is said that every fifth house in Kerala has an expat from the Gulf and every fourth person in the Gulf is a Keralite.

Kerala as a state is low on industrialization and ranks 12th out of India's 16 major states. So, will the returning migrants wait for an opportunity to go back to the Gulf or will they pursue different work. Having got used to a higher pay check, it will be a major social and cultural block to arrest this decline.

On the other hand, nurses are getting employment opportunities in the Gulf all of a sudden due to the pandemic, the state having excelled in handling the public health crisis well enough.

Nurseries, Gardening

People around the world are turning to gardening as a soothing, family friendly hobby that also eases concerns over food security to enable easy availability of crops.

Employees, laid off and on furloughs will have a distraction to grow produces in their own backyards.

Fruit and vegetable seed sales are jumping. Rooftop farms are common in Singapore. With restaurant goers preparing food at home, there would be a need to produce and demand at home. People even plant potatoes in trash bags. Seed demand typically goes up in tough economic times.

Reverse migration and its effects on public health centers and agriculture

The PHC's (Public Health Centers) in India are not adequately staffed. About 60% have only one doctor while about 5% have none according to the Economic Survey 2018-19. More than 10% PHC's in Jharkhand and Chhattisgarh do not have any doctors. More than 90% of PHC 's in Gujarat have only one health doctor. The situation is same with 80% of PHC's in Kerala, Karnataka and 70% of those in Rajasthan, Uttar Pradesh and Bihar.

Doctor per patient ratio. Lack of supplies, inadequate infrastructure facilities, poor monitoring of the staff, etc. may make the reverse migrating population a complex situation of being saddled with high adults whose management will be grossly inadequate.

This is expected to increase the labor costs and impact efficiencies in the medium to long term. Possibly, local labor (plus the return of migrant workers) will help in overcoming labor shortage in many industries. The net impact could be near normal as returning laborers will equal migrant laborers

The Indian Governments ARYA (Attracting and Retaining Youth in Agriculture) scheme is well poised to take off as it could be the ways and means of wooing rural youth to agriculture and allied sectors by ensuring a dignified life in villages. Farm sector can be a respectable profession as besides agro-farming, seed, sapling and allied inputs, etc., one can also manage pump sets to machineries in rural areas so as to boost countryside productivity, etc. With the return of migrants from larger cities, the next one quarter provides an opportunity for the Government to make this scheme click.

Social gathering

Social gathering beyond 20-50 persons may become a rarity for one or more year. Having gone through an upheaval never seen before, would not weddings and gatherings become more frugal. While invites will be lesser, the invitees may desire to give the gathering a go-by considering the circumstances at play.

Restaurants would have reduced the tables by half and only 3 could be seated on a table. In many restaurants, you will be sprayed with disinfectant before entering. Ambience will be different as plastic sheets will be separating each table.

Germany, for instance, allows only 2 families to meet, post the lockdown. Weddings are on hold for an average citizen. For the high and mighty, rules could be different.

State of the marginalized

The marginalized might suffer more, will be humiliated more and marginalized more in a crisis like these. Most of the patients in marginalized societies will live in a state of fear. Whereas in foreign countries, once a person overcomes this virus, s/he will proudly display an immunity certificate.

In countries like India, many neighbors may shun their neighbors or stigmatize their friends just because they may believe that someone could be affected. Fear of being ostracized will run in the minds of any one who returns from a hospital.

Hunger pains are unbearable. In an essay[29] published in a newspaper it is said that in "our straight jacketed bureaucratic imaginations, the

---

[29] Nair Bhaya Rukmini, Essay, The Hindu, Bangalore edition, 03/05/20

poor are conceptualized as mere bodies – that must be fed, clothed and kept healthy, but their individuality is regarded as less than important in a developing society".

Temperature screening

Getting half a dozen temperature checks will now become the new norm.

Be it in your residential/ office/ mall/ airport/ railway/ bus station/ public spaces like super market/ malls/ restaurants, etc.

A high temperature is a sure shot dispatch by ambulance to the nearest hospital and one would not have a choice to decline as rules would be imposed against, by the municipal authorities.

If one is running a simple fever, one may be disallowed to board a train/ airline or enter a shopping mall or any air-conditioned environment.

Many employers would require an employee to take a nucleic acid test before returning to work. One has to leave home with a face mask compulsorily Not wearing a face mask will invite punishment from municipal authority.

Work-From-Home (W-F-H)

Japan as a country is known internationally to be hi-tech but is suffering during this pandemic as they still use fax machines which have become redundant in most countries and employees have not been able to carry out work from home due to non-availability of "hanko"- the official government seal providing notification cum regulation. Similarly, young children and students have been given home works to be carried out and supervised by their parents as teachers are not used to online video education.

Most teachers have called up parents to find out how their wards are performing.

Generally, fewer people commuting to work mean a huge savings of fuel and reduction of road dust. It means less pollution from idling vehicles especially in traffic jams.

One study estimated that a third of America's workforce could work online from home. The Indian proportion would be much less. But the shutdown experience will push corporate India to innovate ways to cut travel, meetings, office space and other activities now considered routine. This will reduce the need for expensive commercial space, airline and train journeys, and hours of commuting time.

Housemaids, construction workers, bus drivers and many other categories of workers cannot function online. But professionals can. New technologies should be developed to enable manual workers to work with equipment that allows social distancing.

Employers will monitor workers with 2 way cameras that will make it possible to monitor the performance of workers and detect absenteeism.

In every role across most organizations, the remuneration will go down by 15-20% with the variable component increasing. Companies will start thinking about paying for work done as opposed to fixed monthly payments in the post Covid-19 era. New tools to measure productivity and collaboration will have to be built.

Technology will disintermediate layers and may flatten organizational hierarchies.

CHAPTER-8
LIFE, HEALTHCARE

Body and mind

The power of prayer and meditation and its effect on the body and mind is immense. Both young and old alike will take a liking to this. It will help people to get a sense of purpose, hope, a positive mind set. The dependence on technology for prayer and faith will not be restricted to millennials.

Edgar Morin, a French philosopher aged 98 years in an interview with Le Monde said "The arrival of this virus should remind us that uncertainty remains an impregnable element of the human condition. "We continue to predict 2025 and 2050 when we are unable to understand 2020".

If we are not in control of the present, how can we predict the future.

Yoga will increasingly be seen as a mind body control in a world where an invisible force can bar us from stepping out of our homes. Possibly gymnasiums will give way to yoga, sitting at home.

Children's health

Many young toddlers feel they were being punished for 40 days of not sending them to school and not allowing them to play with their friends. Many were scared when parents spoke openly about the disease as after all narratives can differ. Children preparing for school examinations got a relief in most classes as they were automatically promoted. Some vying for Board exams were left high and dry with few papers kept hanging in the balance. Some are preparing for State Level Board examinations which seems to come endlessly.

Many of the famed institutes of management and engineering have admitted students based on virtual mediums.

The current uncertainty, coupled with the anxiety that some children's parents are undergoing of poor economy, job loss, etc. would have made them worrisome too.

Climate Change

The pandemic and the climate crisis are both manifestations of nature's response to human activity; one cannot be addressed at the expenses of the other.

Our goal is to limit climatic changes to sustainable levels will require perseverance across economic cycles and political eras. Covid-19 has delivered us a rude awakening to the power of nature operating at its most microscopic level.

Counselling

Mental health support is needed now with work from home, dealing with children, elderly patients and their care, claustrophobia, panic attacks, abuse depression, hypochondriasis, fear of death with the lingering uncertainty around the pandemic etc. Companies will resort to creating an EAP (Employee Assistance Programme) to deal with the mental wellbeing of employees.

Financial priorities, post Covid-19

The income earning capacity of an individual helps one to decide whether to borrow or to save. During good times, a professional may decide to borrow knowing that the current income may not be sufficient to buy a home or a car while another person may decide to create an income buffer to take care of one's income volatility.

Economists believe that there are two ways households react to income volatility depending upon how they read the future as to whether the income shock is temporary or permanent from a psychological or economic perspective:

- If perceived as temporary, they would borrow to protect consumption levels;
- If perceived as permanent, they would increase savings to meet wealth targets.

There is no information to suggest what the Indians may be doing now. Some might have dipped into savings while others may have borrowed through their social circles or could have curtailed their consumption. Income volatility can lead to higher precautionary savings.

Some with steady income might have started increasing their savings. In a published newspaper article[30] it is mentioned that, if the economic pain deepens, one will start increasing savings provided income and assets are more or less intact.

People hold financial assets for 3 reasons:

1. Daily transactions;
2. For speculation (sensitive to interest rate);
3. For precaution.

Those who have lived the Great Depression or the financial crisis remember that savings rate generally increases after a major crisis as the current times. This is especially pertinent for India with the lack of a social security net and lack of income support from any quarter/s.

---

[30] Rajadhyaksha Niranjan, Article, Mint

The effects of the above on macroeconomics are the following:

(I.)   Discretionary spending will come down as a proportion of income as households save more;

(II.)   Demand for bank deposits and government bonds will create space for fiscal expansion till private sector investment picks up;

(III.)   Higher savings will impact the current account balances with the rest of the world.

In the first fortnight of April'2020, Indians moved Rs.1.30. lakh crores from demand deposits to time (fixed) deposits to help it increase to Rs.2.80. lakh crores. Cash holdings have gone up by Rs.41583. crores.

If March '20 is taken for comparison, time deposits stood at 90% which is about 20% higher than the last century's average, the lowest point was after demonetization when citizens went to convert their deposits to exchange old bank notes to new and then the demand deposits swelled.

Savings behavior is a complex exercise. It is dependent on how one sees her income flow for the future and not merely on the current income.

Handwashing – a luxury

Rural India got spared from the Covid-19 but India's rural countryside will be to ensure hygiene and handwashing practices. Official data from NSS (National Sample Survey) suggests that access to water is just 49% and the practice of handwashing is significantly lower in rural areas. Across states, rural areas have lower access in their premises.

Home essentials

Besides consulting a doctor, in order for families to be better prepared to cope with illnesses, minor or major, to monitor ones' health and to alleviate symptoms it is necessary that the following is maintained as a matter of precaution:

a. 30-day supply of prescription medications;
b. First-aid kit;
c. Thermometers – have 2 of them and check fever on both. Wash with peroxide or alcohol;
d. Painkillers- caution is to be exercised here but few painkillers (if allowed vide across the counter sale) can be stocked in limited quantity;
e. Over the counter remedies- throat lozenges, electrolyte replenishes, energy drinks (diarrhoea), antihistamines (seasonal allergies);
f. Safe storage in a cool and dry closet out of the reach of children.

Health and Life Insurance business

India is among the least insured countries and as of 2019, the density of life (which includes health) insurance in the country was a mere 19%, according to data from IRDAI and the biggest reason is the lack of trust. Density is measured as the ratio of premium / total population.

According to Policybazaar.com, health insurance premiums may increase by 5-25% starting October'2020. Life insurance premiums, when taken has a fixed premium during its term while health insurance premiums can vary with inflation.

With an average treatment cost for Covid-19 at about Rs.7.5. lakhs approximately in a private hospital and the communicable diseases not existing or conceived as an occurrence, health insurance premiums were historically low but cannot be maintained in the same pace.

Medical inflation is increasing at double the inflation rate especially with modern technology treatments. Though premiums could go up, one could use cost effective options such as top-ups and family floater plans to enhance ones cover at affordable rates. Having a basic family floater plan with a top-up plan would help meet the need for a higher sum insured. It would be better to get ones' health and life covered soon and if already covered, get them enhanced.

Changes in consumer behavior and rising demand outlook for protection products would lead to higher insurance business. Insurance businesses have generally gone digital.

Past experiences of China and Hong Kong after health scares such as SARS and H1N1 point to strong sales growth potential in the protection segment over the next couple of quarters.

Health care costs are more inclusive than before and high healthcare costs can hurt all of us.

Healthcare Industry

Concern over pandemic and healthcare system

The virus and the state imposed lockdowns have wrought changes that are not just temporary. They will change the world as we have known it most of our lives. We need to learn from the lessons already arising from the diseases and shutdowns, and adopt changes that will take us to a better world.

The foremost lesson is how to better prepare for the next pandemic. Weeks before its outbreak in China, the Bill and Melinda Gates Foundation, along with Johns Hopkins Centre for Health Security and the WEF (World Economic Forum) conducted a high level simulation exercise for pandemic preparedness called 'Event 201', on October 18'2019. They found that the governments, business and public health leaders were all woefully unprepared. Covid-19 has revealed the need to develop resources for future epidemic prevention, and create cost benefit models to evaluate the timing and various types of shutdowns to save lives without excessive economic disruption.

During the pandemic, Nurses, doctors and social workers, the frontline fighters in the battle, have the highest risk of exposure to the virus and have suffered high fatality.

Post Covid-19, countries will create healthcare systems that protect and insulate health workers in fool proof ways. Telemedicine and virtual medicine have been used to a limited extent in many western countries. These need to become universal, used even in the poorest countries that can least afford to suffer a loss of medical staff in the next epidemic.

Government hospitals versus Private hospitals

The healthcare system in the Government hospitals stood up to the tall order of meeting patient requirements and the treatments that followed. Private sector in few states found it difficult to keep pace with the Government hospitals and its methodical working.

The Government medical staff worked for two weeks and took a weeks' break only to return back to work. Sufficient healthcare workers also contributed to the efficacy of the Governmental delivery mechanism at every stage and is generally commended.

Hospitals

The need to quarantine staff at regular intervals, cost of protective gear, diagnostic testing, elective surgeries with falling footfalls will make the hospitals economics badly skewed.

Let me elaborate further, on an average 5 PPEs (Personal Protection Equipment) are used every day for seeing one ICU patient. In addition, every patient who comes to the hospital has to be tested for covid-19. The doctors who see the patient, have to wear PPE assuming that's the patient is Covid-19 positive. Possibly, this is the first time that doctors by and large themselves, being human beings, are scared of contracting the illness.

Private hospitals say their staff expenses alone have doubled in the past one month. Doctors and nurses, dealing with Covid-19 patients, are functioning at 50% of the time as they have to be quarantined for half the month. There is huge backlog of cases waiting for surgery in hospitals.

While the current pandemic definitely has exposed the shortage in ICU bed and staff, we do not think the long term sustainable solution is to just create more beds and increase the staff in proportion. Because the economics of managing the utilization of both infrastructure and costs during the so called "Non-pandemic periods" will make the whole thing unviable on a long term basis (a good comparison is BURN wards). Creation of multiple capacities may not be appropriate.

Soon there will be a demand for technologies that help avoid human contact and as result **Autonomous Vehicles (AV's)** help in delivery of medicines to patients. AV's also help in collection of data that is fed back into the system to improve performance.

Humanoids: In future, humanoids might hand out sanitizers at the reception and collect patient information from visitors. They might have a thermal imaging device to take a patient's temperature vide a contactless thermometer. Upon completion of screening the printouts get generated to a receptionist. A second humanoid then escorts the patient to a waiting room and helps get connected with another robot who in turn connects the patient to a doctor in another room. The robot moves around with the patient to help remote diagnosis.

These in MHO (Medical Health Office), are potentially sustainable solutions in the immediate short terms

I)Creating a pool of ventilators (so that they can be used even during normal times by smaller hospitals etc. - who otherwise struggle for routine emergencies) - solution is operating lease structures;

II)Creating a set of ICU trained staff within the existing staff pool (who like first responders can be immediately redeployed in these emergencies) – this could be offered to government hospital employees first where there is a big shortage

There is little doubt that the government will have to spend to create infrastructure – but to expect private to participate in creating these investment, with socialist pricing, will be a non-starter in our view the challenge is not in the availability of funds / willingness to spend in infrastructure by the government, but in the efficient management of such infrastructure- which is the expertise which private sector can bring.

So a model could be thought of on the following lines:

I)Using funds with pension funds/ LIC etc. to create REIT (Real Estate Investment Trust) to own health infrastructure, long term leases (instead of them investing in stock market/ recovery of failed banks, etc.);

II)Bid out management of project execution (on behalf of the REIT) to private health operators (design etc.)-this will control capital costs;

III)Create a specialty NBFC (Non-Banking Finance Company) to provide equipment finance with a strong Operations and Management SPV (Special Purpose Vehicle) – this is critical to ensure AMC (Asset Management Company), asset rotation, optimization of spares, manpower;

IV) Bid out operations and management of hospitals to private operators;

V)Create in consultation with industry expert's /cost accountants, realistic cost of operations;

VI)Government to fund the cost of operations, thus determined (budgetary support).

Strengthening public health

Healthcare allocation has been a meagre 1.15% of GDP. The public healthcare system had risen to the Corona challenge so far. Possibly, many financial and other resources were diverted to deal with the crisis. Can it sustain in the future?

The private sector accounts for 93% of all hospitals, 64% of all hospital beds, 80-85% of all doctors.

The stimulus package offered by the Government could have created a UHC (Universal Health Coverage) on the lines of most other countries through the public assurance of primary healthcare. India's economic growth can be better done if and only if more financial resources are outlined and earmarked for the country's health infrastructure and strengthening wellness centers, public health service delivery and community health centers. Only then can state governments be better prepared to face subsequent waves of the pandemic.

Home care of senior citizens

Many senior citizens had chosen home care as they were either separated from their families or they chose it as a better option as it was difficult for them to maintain their existing home and its surroundings. However, many in foreign countries suffered as the occupants were staying in close proximity to each other and thereby contracted the illness and suffered immensely to tell a tale and some could not.

 Belgium has been innovative to the extent of having hydraulic cranes moved around the city to help family members to meet their senior citizen parents by getting hauled up to multi storeyed levels in apartment's, so as to show their physical presence and wave or exchange greetings, and to shower their love and affection, in these times as the senior citizens remained confined to their home care centres.

Hunger, Poverty, Homelessness

The world and India, seem to be suffering from the same irony of managing hunger of the deprived by providing food, overcoming poverty with minimalistic means in every form of reaching cash which can buy goods but one does not know where to buy in some of the undeveloped locations. Homelessness, is a serious matter on which Governments around the world have to act quickly as climatic conditions can play havoc on the homeless.

Middle class living

Substitute, replace, adapt is the new mantra.

Middle class citizens before the Covid-19 were a choosy lot. They felt privileged because God had fortunately given them a variety to choose from in their daily lives.

For a Bengali at heart, one is always enamored by the panch mishali: single radish, handful of beans, a layer of cabbage, few leaves of spinach, chunk of pumpkin, a potato, half a cauliflower. This is how frugal you can be while at the same time have a larger variety to suit your palate. Most meat and fish eaters during the Covid-19 became vegetable and egg eaters.

Coconut water, sugar and yeast helps make toddy at home is what my neighbor exclaimed the other day. Just to be a little different one demonstrated the art of making of basic muffins during the lockdown.

Millennials and Gen-X: how are they surviving

Millennials are used to a luxurious lifestyle. They were blessed to have smart phones, electronic gadgets to dictate whatever is happening or is supposed to happen.

Speed of communication, irrespective of the rights or wrongs seemed to be the means of working to an end.

Proficiency in WhatsApp, social media and profiling oneself happened to be the order of the day. Life was a given and the luxuries and comforts inbuilt from childhood. We are referring to the haves and not the have nots.

In our country, the difference between the haves and have nots have only become thinner, post Covid-19.

The millennials were happy goers, enjoyed someone else's companionship, whether physical or digital – WhatsApp call, video call, etc.

Post the lockdown in India, they have become aware of their identity.

The psychological costs of getting through a pandemic can possibly prove to be anxiety ridden leading to depression.

A counselling expert says, "the sudden suspension of a routine provided by a day job can lead to people feeling unmoored. Faced with an existential emptiness, they need to neglect self-care like regular eating, bathing, sleeping, etc."

Many are trying to find the meaning of life, ways to find purpose in their day.

Initially, the lock down was assumed to be a welcome break. With the absence of the maid, cooking and cleaning, all that was a given, with money supply, the questions surfaced as to how life would be, if conditions of current times persisted.

Millennials, at work, felt their work to be the sympathizer and did not have time for their relatives or parents. Now they have started visualizing familial responsibilities and parental care as an essential.

They have started trying out new routines like playing Ludo, conducting quiz, watching sports, films and have stopped depending on what's app forwards. Dating, from physical has become virtual.

Floh, Zoom, etc. are the mediums. These are driving out anxious moments about the disease and diverting one's mind at least for a while.

After all countries have started sifting what's app forwards as fake news. Learning musical instruments and going for something soothing has become the order of the day.

After the lockdown ends, for an introvert, when back in office one shall appreciate meeting one's colleagues more than on ever has.

Technology continues to be a savior for the young millennials. People have started cooking basic microwave meals. People are getting accustomed to a minimalist lifestyle. It has helped one to the virtues of streamlining the needs all over again. Going around, in the future will be considered as a supreme luxury.

For a person born in the 60's, with no television, smart-phone, internet for long periods of time, there never existed a reason to complain in the modern days of Covid-19 as adaptation and being flexible held the key for one's survival. Gen X always found comfort, solace and hope in friendships and dwelled on art, books and music during their spare time. Each generation has been approaching this new normal differently. The baby-boomers hunkered down on their bunkers screaming at the television screens while the Gen X's were frantically erasing the WhatsApp forwards and avoiding fake news but, the millennials continued relentlessly with their work and tried to attain their fiefdom. The hope and belief amongst all the generations was however common, in that, this sudden unwanted pandemic guest leaves us soon.

Possibly, the Covid-19 will change the way we live in the future. One has started saving more than they have spent in the past, fearing tragic days. People will in all likelihood learn to live with basic minimum and will force oneself to change their consumption pattern/s.

Vaccines and human trials[31]

As the world waits with bated breath for a Covid-19 vaccine, it is necessary to know that the controlled group who undergo these trials are at risk themselves. First the vaccines have to be tested to ensure that they are not harmful themselves and then have to be shown to be effective by preventing the inoculated person from picking up the disease. This means that those who get the vaccine may survive sometimes and those who do not get may not. With the limited medical options available in the past to help those infected, obtaining a successful vaccine effectively requires human sacrifice of law as per a published newspaper article.

WHO (World Health Organization)

WHO which has faced criticism in not being able to identify and contain the virus, is now faced with the prospect of carrying out an independent evaluation to study the origin of the pandemic and all countries have welcomed it.

---

[31] Doctor Vikram, Article-Vaccines and human trials, Economic Times, 09/05/2020, pg. -10

CHAPTER-9
CONCLUSION

There are no solutions to managing the crisis evidenced by us, but only trade-offs as said by Thomas Somwell at Stanford University.

Hopefully our country will build trust and confidence in the Government and will invest lot more on our public healthcare system by reducing its allocation to defense and invest into community education and community participation. We also need to bolster infectious disease surveillance.

Our fear and anxiety notwithstanding, we feel as much for the stranded migrants, the elderly without support in old age homes, the disabled and elderly and children who got cranky not knowing the reason behind the confinement, friends who lost their jobs or the doctors and medics who continued to suffer and worked tirelessly to get the patients on recovery track.

It is necessary that we build more equal and resilient society that benefit everyone.

In his book, God has a Dream: A vision of hope for our time, Archbishop Desmond Tutu explains that in the traditional African worldview, a person with Ubuntu (oo-boon- too) was someone with attributes of generosity, hospitality, warmth, compassion and the willingness to share and care.

To be told that "you have Ubuntu" was high praise. It meant that one valued human beings for their intrinsic worth and not for the materialistic worth and one valued the world as one human family thriving on loving, mutuality and interdependence.

Agrima Bhasin, a writer shared the story of "common humanity" behind Ubuntu, a story that has often done the rounds on Internet but is worth repeating.

An anthropologist, who was studying an African community, prepared a basketful of fruits and placed it under a tree. He then asked the children in the village to stand ready behind a line and run when asked "GO" so as to win the prize. To his surprise, when he signaled "GO" all the children held the others hand and ran to collectively win the prize. When asked why they did that, the children while eating the fruits said, "How can anyone of us be happy when the others are sad?"

I am because, we are being the philosophy behind the answer says, Archbishop Desmond Tutu.

Blue skies, birdsongs, trees flowering and fruiting which became an object of reverence recently need to be maintained. Air Quality Index (AQI) becoming good and animals claiming city streets could be a thing of the past once locks open in major economies. All of us who started rooting for the earth to curb ourselves and to save our planet should get going with the same thinking. We hope our frugal living should not change towards wasteful habits and go on a spree of indulgences to overcome pent up demand.

As human being and as a society, we now have learnt valuable lessons over the last 8 weeks, let us continue to practice social distancing but let us not distance ourselves from ideas of empathy, generosity and caring.

Let us hope that we work on an economy that conserves earth resources, avoids future pandemics, and enhances physical and mental well-being.

In the words of Lenin, "there are decades where nothing happens; and there are weeks where decades happen."

L Ravindran and Tara Ravindran

AFTERWORD

Covid-19 has been a black swan event. During the first fortnight of March'2020, after cancellation of all business trips involving flight travel, not realizing what the disease was all about, curiosity got the better of us. With no projections of how the situation would unfold and the safeguards to be taken, every now and then the news emanating from the European countries only added to the confusion. Watching one television channel, a noted economist and an epidemiologist was quick to point out that the disease around the corner will slip the worldwide economy into a major recession, unseen, post the Great Depression. An astrologer was quick to react the next day that a world War like situation was looming large. My mind went into quick thinking to understand what households and countries of this world did to overcome their plight when major tragedies struck in the past several decades ago. Little did we get information, except many statistics, which left us pondering.

We then decided that Covid-19, the event around us, unfolding in front of our eyes should be captured with particular reference to India. We are glad that this book will serve as a ready reckoner for any one lurking with fear of the unintended consequences that may befall us should there be another crisis of this magnitude. This book does not provide any solutions but captures the moment as it is and reveals how humans and Governments brace up to defend themselves. In adversity, lies opportunities!

The children of the next generation will adopt the new found PPE's (Personal Protection Equipment's) and W-F-H (Work from Home) models but what made them to come to this moment should be remembered.

As we advance in life, we learn the limits of our abilities' – Freud

'There is nothing permanent except change' – Heraclitus

'Even if you on the right track, you'll get run over if you just sit there' – Will Rogers

Epilogue

By Aishwarya Ravindran, daughter of the authors

The pre Covid-19, brought out beautiful thoughts of a family bonding but got postponed for reasons as diverse as travelling to quarantining to holding back to be with my employer when most needed by them. The aftereffects of lockdown have brought strict measures on work from home and work at home with personal life interjected with official life. We have started spending more time in front of our computers than ever- as meetings and emails and messages have become the effective communication mode. The fatigue that sets in disallows you to unwind to watch Netflix or to cook.

The authors of this book, my parents, have vividly captured most of the day to day occurrences in our lives so as to be an easy reference, post the pandemic which should pass sometime in the future.

With people getting sick of staying indoors, many have ventured into their passion, be it playing music, listening to podcasts, singing, indoor exercising, dancing, gardening, mask making, cooking, spring cleaning, posting messages in social media, etc.

As authors, my parents have carefully utilized their spare time, after work from home hours, to bring about a book which in my view is likely to be contextual and topical in more ways than one, at least for an Indian. Having said this, living with my parents during my formative years taught me to get energized on how to be empathetic and imagine how other people's lives are like.

L Ravindran and Tara Ravindran

ABOUT THE AUTHORS

L. Ravindran, born, bred in Calcutta (now Kolkata) is buttered in Bangalore (now Bengaluru). With over 3 decades of work experience as a corporate professional, organisation builder and supreme team player and as a first generation entrepreneur for nearly 18 years, he spends his time reading, playing golf and participating in industrial, commercial, professional and societal matters with ease and panache. He was a keen sportsman, a management graduate who utilised his opportunity to complete his Ph.D. in the midst of the financial and economic crisis in 2009. Never to miss an opportunity, in his mid-fifties, he utilised the last 2 months to write on a topical subject of rarity.

Tara Ravindran, born in Tamil Nadu moved around the country being the daughter of a senior Armed Forces official due to which she has seen and experienced many cultures, habits, people and learnt many languages. Trained as environmental sciences student, she went onto pursue Post graduation in management with stellar record. She pursued interior decoration and teaching for few years before embarking as an entrepreneur more than 15 years back. As a Corporate Director, she handles the Finance, Operations and HR functions. She is passionate about gardening, cooking, caring for stray dogs besides few environmental well-being. As an athlete and orator, she excelled during her graduation Writing this book has been a new experience and learning!

The couple have a married daughter who works in the cyber security space.

The authors can be reached at Ravind0099@gmail.com

PRAISE FOR THE AUTHORS

" While the unanticipated, unprecedented deadly Covid-19, engulfed the globe faster than any calamity in history, people and governments tried to respond with fear and anxiety. Dr Ravindran and Ms. Tara teamed to lay everything else to rest, and indulged creatively to present us with ACBC, a rare guide to the past, the present and the changing dynamics of the future". – **Gopal Hosur, IPS, Retd. Inspector General of Police.**

History is based on evidence and relics of the past, blended with conjectures and inferences. Rarely has history been written concurrent with the event. Ravi and Tara, have attempted to write history-life as we know it "Before Corona"-with a twist. They have captured events concurrently as the situation is unfolding on a day to day basis. They have also more daringly tried to pre-empt the likely future-After Corona. -**Hari Narayan Sharma, Corporate professional.**

"If there is any Balance Score Card approach to building a nation, it is right here. An incisive and all-encompassing view on nation building in the new normal Post Covid era " – **Parag Dani, CEO, GAP and Aeropostale- part of Arvind Lifestyle Brands.**

ACBC is a brief inquiry into the changes that have befallen us, with rational insight into how we are likely to cope with COVID19 pandemic in various spheres of our life- a sure snapshot of the present, with a window to the future. - **Dr. Shankar.K, Surgeon.**

Dr. Ravindran and his wife Tara have a boundless energy to live in the moment. The impact of Covid-19 and how the world will change, have been given a deeper thought in this book to what we all have learnt in the last two months and how we can look at a better world as we go ahead. – **Suresh Badami, Executive Director, HDFC Life.**

The authors experiences and observations from an economic standpoint will bring to life the after effects of the sudden halt to our world and its re-emergence. The book is relevant and a must have for the young generations as it explains lucidly the difference between now and the future. – **Tejaswini Ananth Kumar, Trustee, Adamya Chetana.**

Appendix-I

Typical Standard operating procedure (SOP) at Indian airports, post lockdown

- The passengers should reach the airport minimum two hours prior to departure and only those passengers will be allowed to enter the terminal who have their flight scheduled in the next 4 hours.
- All passengers will have to wear protective gear such as gloves and masks.
- All passengers above the age of 14 years of age must be registered on the Aarogya Setu App. The registration on the app is not mandatory for passengers below the age of 14 years.
- Airports to ensure thermal screening before the passenger enters the terminal and only passengers who are marked green on Aarogya Setu can enter the terminal.
- The use of trolleys should be discouraged.

Typical SOP in an Orthopedic practice (post Covid-19)

- Minimize admissions for inpatient care
- Minimize no of patients
- Use telemedicine
- Schedule appointments, avoid unnecessary appointments, talk to patients on phone before calling to OPD/ clinic
- Keep waiting area vacant
- Maintain hand hygiene
- Call minimal staff for work
- One patient, one attendant
- Maintain social distancing
- Patient and attendant to wear masks
- Health care workers should use hand scrubs, masks
- Surgical at least, gloves and hospital shoes
- Should have separate assessment and procedure rooms
- Give one stop treatment, minimal follow up visits
- Avoid interdepartmental referrals, if possible

- Minimum x ray / investigations
- Follow up x rays only when one expects it will have drastic impact of patient's management
- Shift c- arm to OPD (Out Patient Department), to avoid visits to radiology department
- Use videos / online rehab tools for patient rehabilitation

Typical SOP in a hotel, post lockdown

- All touch points in public areas like door handles, elevator buttons, counter tops, table tops, railings, etc. are to be cleaned continuously using a sanitiser/disinfectant. These practices have also to be in place in guest rooms during the morning housekeeping service and at turndown in the evening.

- Electrostatic sprayers with professionally identified chemicals are to be used to disinfect the hotel entrances, employee entrances, as well as various public areas.

- Protocols have to be in place for staff in the kitchens, restaurants, in-room dining, business centres and banquet halls to sanitise their hands every time they serve food or touch food related items.

- Updated and detailed cleaning checklists, including the use of professionally identified chemicals and agents for all areas, including laundry, have to be followed and monitored closely.

- All supplies and materials have to be sanitised before being admitted into the hotel premises.

- Correctly formulated hand sanitisers have to be in place in all guest rooms and at all public spaces and including the entrances, lobbies, corridors, business centres, cloak rooms, etc.

- Cars in hotels meant for guests have to be disinfected after each use, as is luggage, before entering the hotel.

- Masks and disposable gloves have to be worn by all team members at all times and changed frequently. Housekeeping staff shall have to use fresh gloves for every room they service.

- Restaurants and seating in the lobby have to be reconfigured to ensure safe distances are maintained between guests.

- Temperature readings of non-resident guests have to be undertaken at the entrance of the hotel. Temperature readings of resident guests and team members have to be taken up twice a day.

- A guest check-in self-declaration form should be in place which covers COVID-19 symptoms. Any guest who indicates these symptoms is required to undergo a medical examination prior to check-in.

- If any of the parameters for its hotel guests or colleagues are not normal, a medical examination and medical assistance have to be provided immediately.

- Masks, tissues, disposable gloves should have proper waste disposable methods and not mixed with other normal wastes.
- Professional agencies and doctors have to be on standby for sanitisation of all areas should there be anyone detected with a positive sign of COVID-19.

- Detailed Standard Operating Procedures have to kept in place in case of a positive COVID-19 diagnosis where a guest or a colleague needs to be quarantined.

www.ingramcontent.com/pod-product-compliance
Lightning Source LLC
Chambersburg PA
CBHW071619150726
48000CB00004B/1791